Compassion Fatigue

in the

Animal-Care Community

D0873066

by

Charles R. Figley, Ph.D.

and

Robert G. Roop, Ph.D.

THE HUMANE SOCIETY
OF THE UNITED STATES.

HUMANE SOCIETY
U N I V E R S I T Y

8/12

#62897304

Figley, Charles R., 1944–
   Compassion fatigue in the animal-care community / by Charles R. Figley
   and Robert G. Roop.
      p. cm.
   Includes bibliographical references and index.
   ISBN 0-9748400-7-6
   1. Animal shelters–Employees–Job stress. 2. Veterinarians–Job stress.
   3. Animal welfare–Psychological aspects. 4. Compassion. I. Roop, Robert G.
   II. Title.
   HV4708.F53 2006
   636.08'32019–dc22

                                    2005036306

Humane Society Press
An affiliate of the Humane Society of the United States
2100 L Street, NW
Washington, D.C. 20037

Printed on 100 percent post-consumer recycled paper,
processed chlorine free and FSC certified, with soy-based ink.

Charles R. Figley, Ph.D., is Fulbright fellow and professor, and director of the Traumatology Institute, College of Social Work, at Florida State University. He is the author of more than twenty books, including *Compassion Fatigue: Secondary Traumatic Stress Disorders in Those Who Treat the Traumatized* (1995); *Compassion Fatigue: Coping with Secondary Traumatic Stress Disorder* (1995); *Burnout in Families: The Systemic Costs of Caring* (1997); *Brief Treatments for the Traumatized* (2002); and *Treating Compassion Fatigue* (2002), and is the world's foremost expert on the subject of compassion fatigue. He lives in Tallahassee, Florida.

Robert G. Roop, Ph.D., is vice president, Human Resources and Education, for The Humane Society of the United States. He holds a master's degree in community counseling psychology and a doctorate in human resource management. He leads Humane Society University, which offers professional development opportunities to the animal-care and -control community. A certified compassion fatigue specialist, he has taught courses in management at Webster University, Johns Hopkins University, George Washington University, and the Catholic University of America. He lives in the Washington, D.C., area.

For Laura Reeves Figley, who is dedicated to improving the quality of life of all animals, big and small, and for the hundreds of animal caregivers who have so generously shared their journeys of hope and caring with us. Their sincerity and candor have contributed greatly to this effort and have resulted in the writing of *Compassion Fatigue in the Animal-Care Community*.

Contents

Figures

Acknowledgments

I would like to acknowledge the important contributions to our understanding of compassion fatigue made by Zahava Solomon of the University of Haifa, Beth Stamm of the Idaho State University, and Laurie Anne Pearlman of the Traumatic Stress Institute. I sincerely appreciate the support of my daughters, Laura and Jessica, and my wife, Kathy. Deborah Salem has been a critical resource in enabling us to complete this project in a timely manner and in a highly readable form.

Finally, I offer my thanks to all of those in the Green Cross who responded to the needs of animal-care professionals, helping eight thousand animals survive hurricanes Katrina and Rita, especially Incident Commander Dan Casey; Mary Schoenfeldt, operations section chief and site team leader at the Lamar Dixon Expo Center, Gonzales, Louisiana; and those animal-care workers who responded to the critical need in the wake of those horrific disasters.

—*Charles R. Figley, Ph.D.*

I must recognize the encouragement and support of my wife, Mary, who has made this book a reality. Her understanding of the emotional investment this effort required gave me the mental energy to continue. In addition, I want to acknowledge three of my companions who have played a major role in my life and have given me insight into compassion fatigue, J.B., Jezabelle, and Kitten.

I would like to thank Wayne Pacelle, president and CEO of The Humane Society of the United States, for his encouragement, vision, and support of this project.

It is with great pleasure that I acknowledge the efforts of my staff at The HSUS. Their support and hard work have been invaluable. Among the many, two stand out: Lisa Boan, for her excellent proofreading skills and suggestions, and Janet Snyder, for her skilled management of the seminars on compassion fatigue.

—*Robert G. Roop, Ph.D.*

Foreword

Caring for animals is more than a job. For most people who work in the animal-protection field, it's a calling, and along with the rewards come great emotional hardships. Whether you work at a shelter, a sanctuary, or a veterinary clinic, or in one of the thousands of animal-protection groups in America, every day brings a mix of hope and despair. Even on the best of days, there are disappointments and painful moral choices—-and there is always more work to do.

Compassion Fatigue in the Animal-Care Community is a reminder that, unless we are willing to confront the animal suffering, in all its distressing forms, we cannot fulfill our calling to help fellow creatures in need. More than that, as Drs. Charles R. Figley and Robert G. Roop show us, there are practical ways to manage the emotional challenges and press on each day with the hard work of compassion.

Shelter workers and volunteers in particular will find valuable guidance in *Compassion Fatigue in the Animal-Care Community*. They take on shelter work in the hope of savings lives, and often, instead, are filled with grief and guilt at their part in euthanizing animals for whom no space or home can be found. Even while other stray animals are saved every day in those same shelters, it's a terrible emotional burden, and for those who bear it this book is essential reading.

Compassion Fatigue in the Animal-Care Community picks up where William H. Smith left off in his 1990 *Euthanasia: The Human Factor*, the first book to study the psychology of compassion fatigue within the animal-care profession. Figley and Roop have collaborated over the years in workshops and counseling sessions for animal-care professionals throughout the country who are dealing with euthanasia and other emotionally painful circumstances. This practical experience makes their book much more than an academic exercise: they have seen the hurt and sorrow of shelter workers up close and know how deep it runs in the profession.

For years, compassion fatigue was an unspoken occupational hazard of humane work. It caused diminished productivity, high attrition rates among shelter workers, and, worst of all, despair. With scholarship, experience, and empathy, Figley and Roop explain the causes, symptoms, and treatments of compassion fatigue. They stress the importance of self-help and offer specific plans that individuals can easily follow to alleviate or mitigate the symptoms of fatigue.

In the vocation of helping and protecting animals in need, all of us must be smart as well as strong. For thousands of men and women called to serve animals, *Compassion Fatigue in the Animal-Care Community* will be a source of both strength and smart advice. The book cannot remove all the hurts that come with our calling. But it will help every reader to regain hope and do the important work that only we can do.

Wayne Pacelle
President & CEO
The Humane Society
of the United States

Introduction

For several years we have collaborated in leading sessions on stress reduction and other ways to combat compassion fatigue for members of the animal-care community. We've spent many hours poring over journals, books, and websites in an effort to find the most pertinent information for our unique audience. Despite our best efforts, we have been unable to find one source that focused solely on compassion fatigue among animal-care professionals. *Compassion Fatigue in the Animal-Care Community* is designed to fill that void.

This book focuses on the dedicated professionals who care deeply for their work. These animal-shelter workers, managers, veterinarians, veterinary technicians, and veterinary staff continue in their work because they care. In fact, they care so much that their work becomes their lives. While at work these professionals experience joy and satisfaction, but they also experience incredible pain and suffering. Their work—their jobs—hurts, yet they persevere. While there may be several reasons for this dedication, no doubt one is the powerful human-animal bond that ties the worker to the animal. While this bond may bring professionals extreme joy and satisfaction, it also has all the ingredients necessary for development of compassion fatigue in those professionals.

We hope that by explaining what compassion fatigue is and what causes it, how it differs from compassion satisfaction and burnout, and how it is affected by the different types of relationships the animal-care professional develops, we can then introduce the caregiver to the idea of a framework of self-care. We believe this framework of self-care to be the most important part of our efforts to combat compassion fatigue.

Charles R. Figley, Ph.D.
Robert G. Roop, Ph.D.

PART I

COMPASSION FATIGUE: AN OVERVIEW

The Costs of Caring

CHAPTER

"*I am afraid I am not cut out for this work,*" *explained Mary to her supervisor on the second morning of her job at the Miami Rape Crisis Connection (MRCC), in Dade County, Florida.*

She had received her master's degree in social work just a week earlier, and she had completed an internship with the MRCC the previous year. She felt well prepared for the work, which involved providing crisis counseling to rape victims by traveling whenever—and wherever—a victim called for help. Mary had responded to a call at noon the previous day from a thirteen-year-old girl. The police had called the number for the girl after she had given them a description of the suspected rapist, her twenty-two-year-old former "boyfriend."

Mary went on: "I've had similar cases when I interned here, but this one was different. The kid was so scared, and the perp is so scary. I had nightmares all night!"

Mary had found her training as a crisis counselor useful. She loved her job and knew what to do and say. She was familiar with her locality's criminal justice system and law enforcement procedures. She knew the traumatology of rape victims and assessment and treatment strategies. But being an intern under the direction of a staff counselor was very different from being a staff counselor herself. *Also, something about this girl* had struck a chord in Mary deep enough not only to affect her sleep but also to shake her faith in her choice of career.

This book is about you and your work with animals, with their owners, and with those who care for—or hurt—animals. Just as Mary found *her* job to be both rewarding and stressful, so may you.

In this book we tell you about compassion fatigue. We talk about the costs of caring for others and how those of us who work in the animal-care field, in turn, may find ourselves doing so at the cost of our own care. We discuss how empathy is important in the helping process but that by being empathic we can put ourselves at risk. We provide a road map for understanding the territory of helping others, including the most important concepts and their definitions. We hope to show you that the people who are best at helping others are often most vulnerable to compassion fatigue; that compassion fatigue and other unwanted consequences of helping can be prevented; and that, by knowing about compassion fatigue's causes, consequences, and cures, you can help others, as well as yourself, avoid it. We provide a scholarly review of the subject of compassion fatigue for those of you who want a thorough understanding of the costs of caring through a review of what has been learned about compassion fatigue in fields unrelated to animal protection. We also discuss established methods for assessing and treating compassion fatigue.

> Empathy, according to most dictionaries, is the identification with and understanding of another's situation, feelings, and motives.

We now turn to the critical component in helping others—be they animals or human animals.

The Empathy Requirement in Caring

In the example that opens the book, Mary had learned in school how connecting with clients is vitally important in the helping process. Her professors had guided her studies of journal articles and books that review research on the most effective ways to interview, assess, counsel, and otherwise help clients. All of these activities start with establishing and maintaining a "therapeutic alliance," which enables the client to feel comfortable enough with the helper for the helper to gather critical information before any services can be designed and implemented. Comfort involves trust, and both emerge from the initial interactions between client and helper. The vital ingredient to enable the helper to establish trust and comfort is the helper's ability to empathize with the client so that the helper can really know and understand what the client is going through. By doing so, the helper is able, almost without effort, to say and do the right things in the process of helping.

The *Merriam-Webster Medical Desk Dictionary* (2002) defines empathy as

> [I]maginative projection of a subjective state into an object so that the object appears to be infused with it. It is the action of understanding, being aware of, being sensitive to, and vicariously experiencing the feelings, thoughts, and experiences of another of either the past or present without having the feelings, thoughts, and experiences fully communicated in an objectively explicit manner.

Thus, empathy is a response. Saying and doing the right thing nearly effortlessly requires "imaginative projection" and to "be infused with" the person being helped, thereby becoming a fellow traveler with this person in his or her quest to secure help.
At the same time, however, empathy is a process.

Empathy, according to most dictionaries, is the identification with and understanding of another's situation, feelings, and motives. Empathizing is impossible if one does not have the ability to empathize. Intelligence is important but not necessary to this process. Many smart people are unable to guess the thoughts, feelings, and experiences of another after spending some time with that person. Those of us who have empathic ability know it and should feel very fortunate to have this gift.

The Compassion Requirement for Effective Caregiving

Closely associated with empathy is compassion, which is defined as a deep awareness of the suffering of another, coupled with the wish to relieve that suffering. Compassion is a kind of focused empathy, one that is action oriented.

Compassion in animal caregiving requires, in addition to empathy, an *interest* in the animals and their owners. Those working in animal care, however, may have little compassion for those who abuse animals, since to be compassionate is to be interested in such individuals' welfare. This typically is not the case.

Compassionate caregiving requires the act of attending. We may have considerable empathic ability and be compassionate and interested in our clients, but we must also be well trained and attentive to what is happening to them. This requires putting our own feelings and needs aside. Attending in a skilled way enables us to generate trust and forge a connection with our clients. In doing so we are better able to acquire the necessary information to make an appropriate diagnosis and deliver the right kind of services at the right time in the right manner.

Therefore, to establish and maintain a good working relationship with our clients requires a therapeutic alliance that cannot be established without empathy and compassion. Such an alliance enables us to understand what our clients need and want and to be able to help them as much as we can and should. It requires empathy, both as a by-product of our work and in the process of our work. To be empathic requires a basic empathic ability, interest, and attention. But empathy comes with risks and costs.

The Emotional Costs of Caring

Mary quickly discovered that empathy is a double-edged sword. While it was a powerful tool in enabling her to bond with her young rape victim client, it also required her to enter the victim's world—not just to understand but also to experience the fear, shame, conflicts, and other symptoms caused by the traumatic event in the victim's life. The process of fully understanding and embracing the victim's world enabled Mary as a practitioner to help the victim, to bond with her, to gain her trust, and to help her more completely than had she not empathized. Throughout her life, Mary had been well aware of her special gift for empathizing with others—for being able to use the knowledge acquired from her connections with others to say and do things that, although just right at the time, were not part of any particular plan. Mary would describe it as "winging it."

Being a professional caregiver enabled Mary to be paid for doing something she loved and for which she had a gift—helping others. Mary soon discovered, however, that when she entered the victim's world, not as a friend, not as an acquaintance, not as someone she was helping voluntarily, but as a stranger, it was harder. She had to work harder at empathizing, and she had to work harder at letting go of the aftermath. She was discovering the emotional cost of caring as a *professional* caregiver.

Based on an entire career and a decade of research, one of the authors (C.R.F.) (1995, 2002) suggests the following emotional reactions directly caused by our work with the suffering:

- A sense of powerlessness, helplessness, or ineffectualness as helpers
- Anxiety or fear when thinking about the clients' collective plight. This is associated with a sense of apprehension, uncertainty, and even terror that can be traced to anticipation of a realistic or fantasized threatening event or situation facing clients. These events or situations can impair physical and/or psychological functioning.
- Guilt such as that a helper who felt incompetent or responsible for the plight of a client would feel
- Anger or rage either toward those who are responsible for the client's misfortune or toward the client for seeking help
- Survivor guilt—a special sense of guilt associated with those who have survived some catastrophe that took the lives of many others. It is a sense that more could have been done to prevent death or suffering or both.
- Shutdown or numbness—not being able to empathize after a certain point due to exhaustion
- Sadness—affected or characterized by sorrow or unhappiness either directly or indirectly due to the plight of one's clients
- Depression, ranging from clinical depression, characterized by an inability to concentrate; insomnia; loss of appetite; feelings of extreme sadness, guilt, helplessness, and hopelessness; and thoughts of death, to a general and often temporary and distractible state of sadness
- Hypersensitivity, for example, reacting emotionally with little provocation, such as crying easily
- An emotional roller coaster: feeling hypersensitive and sad one minute and angry and hyperactive the next
- Overwhelmed—reaching one's limits in time, patience, and sensitivity expended on others, especially one's clients
- Depleted as a helper—severely weakened by the work of helping others due either to the quality (e.g., intensity or difficulty of the clientele) or quantity (e.g., the amount of time delivering services and/or a high caseload of difficult clients).

The "Competency Costs" of Compassion Fatigue

Mary is not suffering from compassion fatigue yet. The acute compassion stress she feels now could lead to compassion fatigue if something isn't done about it. She is experiencing the initial, emotional costs—the "stings" of caring. Of equal concern are the costs to her competence as a social worker and rape crisis counselor. When we helpers are upset or preoccupied, it limits our judgment and reduces our reaction time. It is impossible to think of two things simultaneously. When we are preoccupied emotionally, our decision making is hampered, due to how the human brain functions.

The Definition of Terms and the Nature of Compassion

CHAPTER

*"**A**re you alright?"*

A Dade County police officer, Officer Jane had slowed down when she noticed Mary's car on the side of the street. Mary had her head down, and when she looked up, her eyes were red. She had been crying. "Oh yes," Mary said, startled. Forcing a smile, she explained that all she needed was some rest. Officer Jane had just left the scene of the crime. Mary had dropped off her client, the victim, Sally, at the local hospital and into the care of a trained nurse and victim advocate. More and more, Mary had become overwhelmed with the fear and distress her clients experienced. It was 10 A.M., and she had been working since 4 A.M. on just five hours of sleep. She was more emotionally exhausted than physically fatigued.

Mary did not tear up when working with Sally or any other client. She worked hard, at times, to keep her real feelings and thoughts hidden from her clients. But working hard and controlling her emotions led to mistakes. To be more effective at managing her distress and enjoying her job, she needed a lesson in the way her brain operated.

The Neurobiology of Compassion Stress

Mary, like all of us, is susceptible to the way we are wired and programmed neurobiologically as human beings. In the mid-1970s, it was discovered that all human brains have two hemispheres, left and right. The practical application of this knowledge is emerging more slowly than is the scientific progress, so some background may be helpful in fully appreciating the professional toll compassion fatigue takes on the human mind.

Each hemisphere of the brain is dominant for certain behaviors. For example, it appears that the right hemisphere is dominant for spatial abilities, face recognition, visual imagery, and music. The left hemisphere may be more dominant for calculations, math, and logical abilities.

There is a tendency for the two cerebral hemispheres to operate in two very different contexts, one emotional and the other rational. For right-handed people, the left hemisphere is the dominant one for verbal/logical thinking and the details so important to professional functioning. The right hemisphere dominates in the non-verbal/intuitive functioning that involves philosophical, holistic patterns of thinking. Thus, it is knowledge versus knowing. We need both, and when we are not in a distressed state of mind, both hemispheres work collaboratively, as they are intended. What makes this possible is the *corpus callosum*, a very important bundle of nerve fibers located between the two hemispheres that serves as a neural pathway or gate.

This is where we introduce you to Molly.

Molly could not stop thinking about an episode at the clinic three days ago. It was now Sunday evening, and she would be returning to the "scene of the crime." The more she thought about it, the more upset she became. She was especially annoyed because it was not the first time a patient had died in her arms. But the look on that child's face when it happened! She was expecting Molly to save her little dog, and when the dog went lifeless, she screamed. The look and the scream had stuck with Molly ever since.

During exposure to a shock like this, Molly's brain initiates a cascade of automatic neurobiological responses. Glucocorticoids[1] are released to mobilize energy, increase cardiovascular activity, and slow unnecessary physiological processes. Molly's heart had immediately begun to race, and she found herself turning around with the dog and going into the surgery. She knew the dog was dead and that she could do nothing for her. She just wanted to get away from the screaming and the look on the child's face. When Molly remembered the event—either voluntarily or involuntarily—she felt the same sensations. It was as if her body reactions were synchronized to her memory.

When Molly or anyone else is exposed to shocks that continually generate extremely high levels of glucocorticoids, it could lead to major medical problems, including hippocampal volume reduction[2] (Boscarino 2004).[3] Continued exposure to extreme or chronic traumatic events or the memory of them can result in abnormal patterns of neurotransmitter and hormonal activity and in permanent changes in neuronal differentiation and organization.[4] Therefore, both primary and secondary trauma need to be taken seriously and deserve immediate attention.

The Social Psychology of Compassion Stress

In addition to the neurobiological effects of compassion and secondary stress are the social psychological causes and effects. Both Mary and Molly derive a good part of their joy and sorrow in life from their interactions with others. The social psychology of compassion fatigue is an appreciation of the manner in which the *personality, attitudes, motivations,* and *social relations* of the individual affect work-related stressors, especially the capacity for managing compassion stress.

Personality and Compassion Stress. The personality of Molly—or of any other animal-care worker—includes the totality of qualities and traits that make her special, her style and approach that remain consistent across situations and time. Some workers are like a cork in a turbulent creek, sometimes going under the water or bumping into a rock, but always bobbing back to the surface. Other workers may be more like paper boats, far less resistant to the jostling of the same turbulent creek. Research on resiliency, hardiness, and optimism has found that these traits appear to be associated with happiness across situations. Thus, animal workers who tend to be viewed more like the cork discussed above are more likely to "roll with the punches" of the ups and downs of animal-care work.

Attitudes, Motivations, and Compassion Stress. Animal-care workers who have positive attitudes toward their work and are motivated by such attitudes will experience greater satisfaction. Work satisfaction is a critical element in preventing and overcoming the stresses of work, including compassion stress. Positive attitudes and motivations sometime emerge with time and training; however, in most instances a positive attitude emerges at the beginning of one's career. Understanding the "calling" of animal care, therefore, is a critical factor in predicting and managing compassion stress, because no matter how bad the medical emergency, no matter how distressing or upsetting the event at the time, the animal professional's attitude and sense of motivation are a critical salve for the traumatic wound. This is in contrast with someone who seeks out a particular career mostly for money, prestige, or power.

Social Relations, Social Support, and Compassion Stress. The final set of factors associated with compassion stress is interactions with colleagues, clients (pet owners), and personal supporters. Each of these groups of people can affect the overall emotional climate of the animal caregiver. In the context of work, compassion stress is a function of the general morale and supportiveness of fellow workers, especially the supervisor and administration. A positive work environment includes workers who care about each other and show it. They genuinely like one another, and they may joke around and/or pitch in when needed and often without being asked to do so. They pick up on even the most subtle mood changes of fellow workers and ask about them in a caring and supportive manner. A negative work environment, on the other hand, is emotionally toxic. Relationships among workers, and especially with supervisory staff, are strained, and staff morale tends to be negative. What is lacking in a toxic work environment is a sense of trust, optimism, and mutual support among and between staff members. As with other social psychological components, the vital resources of supportive colleagues, friends, and family enable the animal-care professional to rebound from emotionally upsetting events.

Concepts and Definitions

We now turn to an overview of the important concepts relevant to understanding, discovering, facing, and overcoming the factors leading to compassion fatigue. Compassion, as noted in chapter 1, is defined as a *deep awareness of the suffering of another coupled with the wish to relieve it.* It is a kind of focused, action-oriented empathy. Fatigue, as we use it here, is the *mental weariness resulting from exertion* that is associated with attending to the emotional and physical pain of others. Stress is a sense of demand for action. When we feel stress, we sense that action is demanded of us—in this case, helping clients. Animal-care professionals experience compassion stress when they feel the demand to help—no matter whether it is real or imagined, possible or impossible. Compassion stress is the demand to be compassionate and effective in helping. Animal-care professionals experience compassion fatigue when they are traumatized by trying to help. Compassion fatigue is exhaustion due to compassion stress, the demands of being empathic and helpful to those who are suffering. Compassion fatigue is a form of post-traumatic stress disorder (PTSD). PTSD is caused by a traumatic event or series of events that can happen to animal workers in the course of their work. The symptoms of PTSD include reexperiencing the event(s), avoiding reminders of the event(s), and physical distress while recalling the event.

> Work satisfaction is a critical element in preventing and overcoming the stresses of work, including compassion stress.

Vicarious trauma is another name for the stressor event, and countertransference is another name for the discomfort felt when confronting the event. The classic definition is the psychotherapist's own repressed feelings in reaction to the emotions, experiences, or problems of a person undergoing treatment. Occasionally animal-care professionals find that a certain animal or owner may awaken "repressed" or forgotten feelings associated with a pet or person in their lives.

Collectively, these concepts are the signposts on our map for understanding and doing something about compassion fatigue, either for ourselves or for our work environment. The model we discuss next describes the problem of compassion fatigue and points to useful solutions. It also suggests that only compassionate, empathic, loving, and caring people suffer from compassion fatigue—the very people who are so vital to the animal-care field.

Putting It All Together

A way of representing the various critical factors accounting for compassion fatigue is included in Figure 2.1; consider it a road map.

This model suggests that the route to compassion fatigue is by way of numerous distressing and "toxic" circumstances. Compassion stress and fatigue among animal-care workers emerges from particularly toxic situations that started with genuine concern and caring on the part of such workers. Empathic ability is the innate ability to empathize with another, be it pet or owner. With this ability animal-care professionals are able to provide the necessary empathic response in their work, to feel the emotional needs and experiences of the animal, pet owner, or both. However, to provide the necessary empathic response—sensitivity, caring, and professionalism—animal-care workers must be concerned for and exposed to the animal and the pet owner. A clear sign of compassion fatigue is the urge to avoid, or the act of avoiding, exposure to the animals and owners who have caused distress in the past and may do so again. Exposure to the suffering, together with effective empathic ability and concern for the suffering, are the necessary ingredients for the animal-care worker to provide the necessary empathic response, given the right kind and amount of training and supervision.

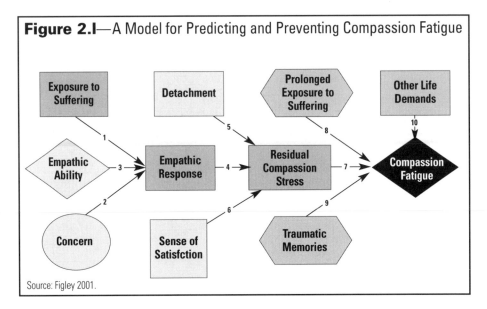

Figure 2.1—A Model for Predicting and Preventing Compassion Fatigue

Source: Figley 2001.

Working day in and day out with suffering animals and owners takes a toll, especially on those who dispense compassion and empathy. There is a cost to caring for the animal-care provider in the form of compassion stress. As noted earlier, and like other forms of stress, stress reactions affect all aspects of human experience and functioning. Eventually the cumulative stress results in compassion fatigue, a form of burnout and PTSD. Two factors reduce compassion stress and, therefore, compassion fatigue. One is compassion satisfaction, a sense of fulfillment or gratification from the work. For animal-care providers it is the joy of helping helpless animals, literally bringing them back to life at times, and the delight in satisfying the desperate needs of a pet owner. Sometimes animal-care workers need to remember these very real satisfactions when feeling the weight of compassion stress from the job.

The other major factor in reducing compassion stress is detachment—psychological and physical—from the job and its stressors. This means more than "having a life" and enjoying it apart from the job while away from it. It also and especially means being able to manage the compassion stress of the job. Later in the book we discuss detachment strategies at work to help recharge your batteries and some ways of doing so away from work.

Three other factors contribute directly to compassion fatigue. One is the prolonged exposure to suffering when an animal-care worker puts in far too many hours without a sufficient break. Sometimes this is unavoidable—when there is a local catastrophe or crisis that requires extensive time working with animals and owners suffering acutely, especially in the case of a natural disaster. Sometimes it is a temporary requirement of the job due to understaffing. Sometimes, however, prolonged exposure is self-imposed by the worker: skipping lunch, delaying vacations, working overtime, and other extensions of normal workloads. Another factor or "road" directly connected to compassion fatigue on the trauma map is traumatic memories. These are the unresolved conflicts and distress associated with remembering a traumatic event, especially with the suffering of others, such as animals, in one's past. The memories are often evoked when workers are empathically engaged with their suffering client owners. There is a tendency either to shut down emotionally out of self-protection or to overgeneralize personal experiences and "overpromote" specific coping strategies found to be useful to the survivor/therapist.

The final factor that contributes to compassion fatigue is the "other" category: other life demands. Often these demands have little to do with the job and everything to do with being stressful. Even positive activities such as getting a new car or falling in love demand time and attention and therefore restrict the resources needed to cope with work. More often, however, other life demands are negative, caused by personal issues, such as family obligations.

Collectively these eleven factors, or roads, lead to compassion fatigue. There are alternative roads leading to alternative destinations, however. They address ways of transforming compassion fatigue into opportunities for change that enable animal-care workers to be far more productive, useful, and happy at work and at home. We explore these in the following chapters.

Four Phases of Adjustment to Being a Helper

Doug Fakkema would love to talk to Mary, and especially to Molly.[5] He has formulated a four-phase explanation for Mary's journey (Fakkema 1991). Others have talked about the struggles of new social work professionals (Sze and Ivker 1986; Samantrai 1992; Dollard, Winefield, and Winefield 2003), human service workers (Tracy et al. 1992; Todd and Deery-Schmitt 1996); nurses (Tai, Bame, and Robinson 1998); and medical professionals (Hilfinker 1985). Based on these perspectives, we offer a five-phase transition period for the new helper. The phases correspond to running (and finishing) a twenty-six-mile marathon, comparable to the first few years of a helping professional's career.

Phase One: The Dream
The helping professions, including animal-care workers, are no different from any other in attracting young people who have dreams of doing well for themselves in their careers. What is different in the helping fields is that our satisfaction comes not only from our own evaluation and the evaluation of our supervisors, but also from how well we think we are doing in helping our clients. Dreams of helping emerge early, perhaps when we are children. We imagine the good work we will do to make a difference in the lives of our clients. Dreams sustain us through our lives and into college and postgraduate education and through our internship. Being dreams, however, they must end, and we eventually must wake up to reality. Although we read about rude

awakenings, as you will do here, it is all theoretical to us, thank goodness! Otherwise, fewer people would join us in the work we do.

Phase Two: The Start

Graduating from school, at any level, and starting our careers is exhilarating. We're on the mark, and once that whistle blows, opponents had better move aside. We're ready to run the marathon and make the world a better place. Fakkema (1991) talks about this phase in the context of animal welfare professionals:

> Red hot and raring to go, we are out to change the world. We are high on life (or at least our job). We know we can make a difference, that our efforts on behalf of animals will ease their plight. We work what seems like 25-hour days yet are energized. Our enthusiasm overflows; our capacity for challenges is limitless. We eat, sleep, and live in the cause for animals. (n.p.)

Phase Three: Losing Our Breath

The first time we run in a marathon provides a greater lesson than can any training or reading. Eventually it sinks in that we have many miles to run. Our enthusiasm dampens, and our resolve begins to diminish. The same is true the first year on the job. We discover there are clients we don't like, supervisors who take the credit for our work, and colleagues who undermine our mission. Emotions run rampant. We feel mad, then angry, and eventually hopelessness prevails. The bubble has burst and set the stage for compassion fatigue symptoms to take charge.

Phase Four: Desperately Seeking Rhythm

In this phase we recognize that, if we want to continue to run, we need to pace ourselves. We need to find a rhythm that works for us, one that sustains our sanity, health, and energy level. Again, the same is true in our jobs. To find our career rhythm, we might need to slow down, take a look around, and devise a plan. Either we are going to take the necessary steps to move forward and complete the marathon, or we're going to check out. Finding our rhythm in running or in our professional lives takes time and experimentation.

> The other major factor in reducing compassion stress is detachment—psychological and physical—from the job and its stressors.

Phase Five: Finding Our Rhythm

As with the first time a lightbulb "goes off"—when learning to read, compute statistics, or ride a bike—finding our pace, our niche, our way is thrilling and provides a sense of relief. We have hit a stride that carries us to the finish line. This doesn't mean that the next marathon is going to be a piece of cake. It just means that now we know better what to expect and have the experience of our previous successes to draw from. It is in this final phase of our jobs that we pay homage to the enormity of the challenges facing our caregiving mission. We begin to see the big picture and where we fit in. In his understanding of the final phase, Fakkema (1991, n.p.) writes of animal welfare professionals:

> We understand and accept that sadness and pain are a part of our job. We stop stuffing our feelings with drugs, food, or isolation. We begin to understand that our feelings of anger, depression, and sadness are best dealt with if we recognize them and allow them to wash over and past us. We recognize our incredible potential to help animals. We are changing the world.

Notes

[1] Any of a group of steroid hormones, such as cortisone, that are produced by the adrenal cortex; are involved in carbohydrate, protein, and fat metabolism; and have anti-inflammatory properties.

[2] Gilerton et al. (2002) compared twenty-six Vietnam veterans with post-traumatic stress disorder (PTSD) to twenty-two normal veterans, similar in age, sex, race, years of education, socioeconomic status, body size, and years of alcohol abuse. Combat veterans with PTSD had a statistically significant 8 percent smaller right hippocampal volume and a statistically insignificant 4 percent smaller left hippocampal volume.

[3] As evidenced by hippocampal degeneration that includes volume loss. The hippocampus contains a high concentration of glucocorticoid receptors. Repeated high levels lead to permanent loss of glucocorticoid receptors in the hippocampus as well as significant damage to the hippocampal neurons.

[4] Neurobiological effects are evident in brain stem dysregulation, alterations within the central nervous system, irregularities in cortical function, alterations within catecholamine systems, and dysregulation of the hypothalamic-pituitary-adrenal (HPA) axis and the hypothalamic-pituitary-thyroid axis.

[5] Doug Fakkema is associate director of training and special projects for the American Humane Association. Fakkema has given workshops addressing humane animal euthanasia and how to deal with its emotional consequences for thirty years. Throughout that time, he has witnessed a "career evolution" so distinct that he came up with four phases. Our formulation is based in part on this formulation.

Work-Related Distress: A Primer on Compassion Fatigue

In this chapter we more thoroughly investigate the nature of work-related mental health, particularly burnout, secondary stress and stress reactions generally, and especially compassion fatigue among animal-care providers.

Work-Related Distress

Work-related mental health problems are one of the main challenges currently facing organizations, particularly because of their serious consequences for the organizations themselves and for individuals. Indeed, a direct link has been found among stress and heart disease, dissatisfaction at work, accidents, and certain forms of cancer. Work-related mental health problems are the primary cause of the increase in absenteeism rates. Not until the 1970s was there sufficient awareness of and some degree of attention given to workplace distress. Historically, work-related stress was perceived to be a problem only in high-pressure, low-paying jobs, such as teaching and social services.

Work-related stress is *not* a weakness, and workers don't have to suffer with it. Employers have a duty to protect their workers' health and safety at work, and a good employer appreciates any employee suggestions for reducing work-related stress. Such stress is a symptom of an *organizational problem,* not an individual weakness.

Work-Related Stressors

For the animal-care provider, examples of work-related stressors are endless.

- *Demands of the job of animal care.* Frequently this means having too much to do in too little time. It can also mean inadequate training and/or supervision or support for caring for animals and dealing with the public. On rare occasions it means boring or repetitive work or having too little to do.
- *Stressors of lack of clarity about responsibilities.* This frequently means feeling confused about how everyone on the staff fits in and/or having responsibility for looking after certain clients and owners.
- *Stressful relationships with fellow animal-care providers.* These include poor relationships with others (e.g., personality clashes, not feeling respected) or being bullied or the target of racial or sexual harassment.
- *Balancing work and home.* Sometimes this means having to deal with inflexible work schedules or emergency calls after hours, or when one's personal life affects work performance. Working conditions stressors include being in physical danger from aggressive or sick animals or owners or being exposed to poor, unhealthy, and even dangerous working conditions (e.g., unsafe neighborhood or physical plant).

> Work-related stress is *not* a weakness, and workers don't have to suffer with it.

- *Stressors caused by management* (departmental supervisors, executive director, or board of directors). Among these stressors are the lack of control over one's own schedule, work activities, and/or immediate environment; a lack of clear and consistent messages and decisions; a negative work culture; and the lack of rewards or support for successes. These chronic stressors on the animal-care worker can lead to a wide variety of negative outcomes, including workplace burnout.

Burnout in the Workplace

Burnout is defined most often as exhaustion of physical or emotional strength, usually as a result of prolonged stress or frustration. The concept of burnout emerged in the mid-1970s as a mental health issue. Work burnout doesn't occur overnight however, unless the distress at work is addressed—no matter the cause, symptoms worsen and become harder to treat. Work-related burnout as a term was coined by Furstenberg (1978), but major developments emerged with the work of Maslach (1982). Work-related burnout is not limited to those who work with the traumatized, and it is as debilitating as in other fields. Burnout can be caused by conflict between individual values and organizational goals and demands, an overload of responsibilities, a feeling of having no control over the quality of services provided, awareness of little emotional or financial reward, a sense of a loss of community within the work setting, and inequity or lack of respect at the workplace (Maslach and Leiter 1997). Often the individuals who experience burnout are highly idealistic about helping others (Pines and Aronson 1988). Burnout also can be related to consistent exposure to traumatic material (Aguilera 1995).

Similar to secondary traumatic stress (STS), discussed later, burnout is a "process, not an event" (Farber 1983b, 3) "marked by physical, emotional, and behavioral indicators that can be easily recognized" (Aguilera 1995, 269), allowing for self-initiated intervention if the caregiver is trained and aware of the manifestations. The physiological responses include physical exhaustion, headaches, and hypertension. Not unlike STS, reactions to burnout include emotional exhaustion (Prosser et al. 1996), depression, and anxiety. Behavioral responses include boredom, decline in performance, insomnia, increased addictions or dependencies, interpersonal difficulties, and cognitive response such as self-doubt, blame, and general disillusionment (Farber 1983a; NiCarthy, Merriam, and Coffman 1984; Prosser et al. 1996). There can be a sense of reduced personal accomplishment and purpose; feelings of helplessness and hopelessness (Maslach 1982); impairment of family relationships (Farber 1983a); development of a negative self-concept and negative attitudes toward work, life, and other people; and nightmares (Pines and Aronson 1988).

The Etzion (1984) study explored the relationship between burnout and social support, since social support has been proposed as a major resource to reduce harmful consequences of stress. Burnout was found to be significantly and positively correlated with stressors, while support is significantly and negatively correlated with burnout. Life support was more effective in moderating work stress for women, while work support was a more effective moderator for men. Women had significantly higher burnout and life stress than men, but enjoyed higher life support.

Prosser et al. (1996) reported that higher rates of burnout were found in community mental health workers than in hospital-based staff. Practice implications addressed the need to develop measures of prevention of burnout, especially for community mental health workers, and for the need for a greater understanding of the impact of long-term involvement on professionals and clientele. Stav, Florian, and Shurka's 1987 study identified frequency and satisfaction of supervision as potential moderators of burnout in social workers in various settings.

For the purposes of this book and our focus on animal-care providers, the symptoms can be organized into five categories: poor motivation, workplace dread, alienation, aggression, and health problems.

Poor motivation. The reasons we choose a job are the same reasons we run from it. Most animal-care workers remember feeling motivated and ambitious at the beginning of their careers or employment. If you do as well, compare that with how you feel today. If you no longer care about doing an exemplary job, if your only aim is to get out of the office as early as possible, or if you find yourself doing only the minimum amount of work you can get away with—with no desire to advance yourself—you may have one of the symptoms of work burnout.

Workplace dread. There are many ways in which your work situation can become intolerable. You may dislike your boss, feel overloaded with work, resent that you are unappreciated, or think all of your clients are difficult to deal with. You may feel that your job is no longer challenging and your tasks have become mundane and repetitive. Feeling that you are stuck in a dead-end job can be demoralizing and can easily lead an animal caregiver to lose enthusiasm for his or her work. This feeling of dislike is also associated with work burnout.

Sense of alienation. Have you begun to feel isolated from your colleagues at work? Do you avoid social contact or conversation with them? Have you begun to resent their good humor or ambition? Mentally separating yourself from work colleagues and others creates a sense of alienation. Animal-care providers in this situation often begin feeling left out (everyone else seems to like his or her job, why don't I?), and these feelings only exacerbate other frustrations.

Aggression. Do you find yourself losing your temper faster than before? Does everything seem to get on your nerves? Animal-care providers who experience symptoms of work burnout often find that they have no patience for what they perceive as incompetence of others. They often want to—or do—snap at colleagues. All this, of course, only leads to further isolation in the workplace.

Health problems. Work burnout eventually manifests itself in some physical form. It is at this stage that most people finally recognize or admit that something may be wrong. The most common health symptoms are tension headaches, backaches, and other stress-related problems. Animal-care workers may also find that they cannot sleep. They may gain or lose weight and find that they are indulging in alcoholic beverages more than usual. Feelings of self-pity or depression are also common.

Systemic Traumatology and Secondary Victimization in Families

People can be traumatized either directly or indirectly (Figley 1982, 1995). *Secondary or systemic trauma,* most often found in the context of families, occurs when the victim is traumatized through the process of learning about the primary trauma experienced by a loved one or by the secondary victim's frequent interactions with a primary trauma victim and his or her presentation of primary trauma symptoms. In contrast to a family member who is in harm's way, other family members may become traumatized by *helping* the family member in harm's way. Therefore, while the symptoms associated with primary and secondary trauma are remarkably similar, there is one fundamental difference.

Secondary Traumatic Stress Reactions

Animal-work practitioners, though not directly in harm's way, show the classic symptoms of post-traumatic stress disorder (PTSD). As noted elsewhere (Figley 1995, 2002), the psychiatric symptoms of people directly in harm's way (e.g., those hit by a car) are called *primary trauma survivors.* They are different from their caregivers, who are exposed to trauma indirectly. *Primary* trauma survivors with PTSD struggle to make sense of trauma memories. *Secondary* trauma survivors (caregivers) try to help primary trauma survivors (i.e., victims) with empathy and compassion and frequently experience symptoms similar to those of the victims. This is secondary or systemic trauma.

Family members report experiencing emotional, cognitive, and behavioral symptoms similar to those reported by the primary trauma victim (Table 3.l). Barnes (2004) reports that the symptoms of secondary trauma reported in the literature include intrusive thoughts, nightmares, flashbacks, feelings of detachment and estrangement from others, restricted affect, avoidance of activities that remind them of the traumatic event, sleep disturbances, hypervigilance, and fatigue. It is clear that traumatized individuals, couples, and families can have a variety of problems that may or may not be presented initially to a health-care professional as being associated with a traumatic event and its post-traumatic aftereffects. Often problems seem to focus on the behavior of other family members or to be marital or couples' issues that are consistent with secondary trauma rather than the primary post-traumatic symptoms of the trauma victim. This situation is often seen following an automobile accident or recovery from a life-threatening illness, such as cancer or a cardiac condition, after which family members experience symptoms they fail to connect with the original traumatic event. A good assessment of past traumatic events, including accidents and medical problems, is important for a health care professional to identify issues that underlie the surface problems.

Compassion Stress and Fatigue

"**C**ompassion fatigue" was first used in discussions related to burnout in nurses exposed to traumatic work-related experiences (Joinson 1992). Nurses who are compassionate are far more than just empathic, according to Koerner (1995).

Table 3.1—The Personal Impact of Secondary Traumatic Stress

Cognitive	Emotional	Behavioral
Diminished concentration	Powerlessness	Clingy
Confusion	Anxiety	Impatient
Spaciness	Guilt	Irritable
Loss of meaning	Anger/rage	Withdrawn
Decreased self-esteem	Survivor guilt	Moody
Preoccupation with trauma	Shutdown	Regression
Trauma imagery	Numbness	Sleep disturbances
Apathy	Fear	Appetite changes
Rigidity	Helplessness	Nightmares
Disorientation	Sadness	Hypervigilance
Whirling thoughts	Depression	Elevated startle response
Thoughts of self-harm or	Hypersensitivity	Use of negative coping
harming others	Emotional roller coaster	(smoking, alcohol or other
Self-doubt	Overwhelmed	substance abuse)
Perfectionism	Depleted	Accident proneness
Minimization		Losing things
		Self-harm behaviors

Spiritual	Interpersonal	Physical
Questioning the meaning of life	Withdrawn	Shock
Loss of purpose	Decreased interest in intimacy	Sweating
Lack of self-satisfaction	or sex	Rapid heartbeat
Pervasive hopelessness	Mistrust	Breathing difficulties
Ennui	Isolation from friends	Aches and pains
Anger at God	Impact on parenting	Dizziness
Questioning of prior religious	(protectiveness, concern	Impaired immune system
beliefs	about aggression)	
	Projection of anger or blame	
	Intolerance	
	Loneliness	

Impact on Professional Functioning

Performance of Job Tasks	Morale	Interpersonal	Behavioral
Decrease in quality	Decrease in	Withdrawal from	Absenteeism
Decrease in quantity	confidence	colleagues	Exhaustion
Low motivation	Loss of interest	Impatience	Faulty judgment
Avoidance of job tasks	Dissatisfaction	Decrease in quality of	Irritability
Increase in mistakes	Negative attitude	relationship	Tardiness
Setting perfectionist	Apathy	Poor communication	Irresponsibility
standards	Demoralization	Subsume own needs	Overwork
Obsession about	Lack of appreciation	Staff conflicts	Frequent job changes
details	Detachment		
	Feelings of		
	incompleteness		

Source: Figley 1995.

Compassion, a prerequisite for their job, is "based on a passionate connection...Passion moves one beyond feeling and emoting toward social action aimed at relieving the pain of others" (317). Koerner further states that having a compassionate style of practicing "demands risk coupled with a recognition of our own limitations" (317). The terms compassion stress and compassion fatigue began to be used synonymously with STS and PTSD, because compassion-fatigue reactions parallel a PTSD diagnosis, except that the traumatic event is the *client's* traumatic experience that has been shared in the process of therapy or interaction with the client.

> Traumatized individuals, couples, and families can have a variety of problems.

Most of the literature on compassion fatigue, however, has focused on psychotherapists who work with traumatized patients. In one of the earliest investigations, Hollingsworth (1993) assessed the responses of therapists working with female survivors of incest as part of her doctoral dissertation. The purpose of the investigation was to build a theory of the effects of such work on female therapists. All of the research participants had experienced lasting negative change in at least one of the following cognitive schema ("an abstracted knowledge structure, stored in memory, that involves a rich network of information about a given stimulus domain" [Janoff-Bulman 1989, 115]): trust of others, safety of children, intimacy, connectedness, esteem for others, and independence of power. General themes indicated included feelings of anger, disgust, sadness, and distress; difficulty maintaining relationships and boundaries; somatic responses; and intrusion symptoms. What Hollingsworth found was instructive. Effective strategies evolved for these female therapists that enabled them to work with this population of clients. These strategies included peer support, supervision and consultation, training, personal therapy, maintaining balance in one's life, and setting clear limits and boundaries with clients. In addition, the study determined the existence of lasting positive changes, which had not been addressed in the literature at that time.

Many competent caregivers are "most vulnerable to this mirroring or contagion effect. Those who have enormous capacity for feeling and expressing empathy tend to be more at risk of compassion stress...resulting from helping or wanting to help a traumatized or suffering person" (Figley 1993, 1). If the signs of STS are ignored, secondary traumatic stress disorder (STSD) may develop. Caregivers with compassion fatigue begin to dream their clients' dreams, experience intrusive thoughts or images (Cerney 1995), and/or experience distress or physiological reactions to reminders of that client's traumatic experience. Symptoms may be exhibited as active efforts to avoid thoughts, feelings, activities, and situations that remind one of the client's traumatic events. There could be a decrease in interest in activities that once brought pleasure or relief of stress; affect can be diminished as well. Compassion fatigue evokes hyperarousal symptoms such as sleep disturbances, difficulty concentrating, high startle response, feelings of agitation or irritability, or hypervigilance (Figley 1995).

Compassion fatigue can affect not only caregivers, but their family and closest friends as well, because they are a system of support (Cerney 1995). The "contagion effect" (Figley 1993) can be transmitted to the support system. Caregivers "may traumatize their families by their chronic unavailability and emotional withdrawal, perhaps in the same way that trauma victims sometimes traumatize those around them" (Cerney 1995, 140). This distancing may occur when caregivers do not believe anyone would be able to understand the distress they are experiencing as a result of such intense and difficult work (Dutton and Rubinstein 1995).

> Compassion fatigue can affect not only the caregivers, but their family and closest friends as well.

Research on compassion fatigue has suffered from conceptual and methodological limitations. Conceptually, researchers have attempted to differentiate compassion fatigue from job burnout, vicarious trauma, and general psychological distress, but the terms have remained imprecise (Jenkins and Baird 2002; Salston and Figley 2003; Sabin-Farrel and Turpin 2003). There has also been little research on how compassion fatigue relates to a history of trauma, social support, coping strategies, or the stress process in general (Schauben and Frazier 1995; Kassam-Adams 1999; Salston and Figley 2003). Lack of conceptual clarity has hindered implementation and measurement of these concepts and impaired empirical development. Several compassion-fatigue scales have been proposed, but there have been few validation studies, with almost no information on the psychometric properties of the scales used (Figley 1999; Gentry, Baranowsky, and Dunning 2002; Stamm 2002).

Previous studies have also often failed to include a comparison group that has *not* been exposed to traumatized clients (to control confounding variables such as the counselor's own trauma experiences), to examine organizational or other factors that may increase the vulnerability of a therapist to compassion fatigue, and to implement research to assess the causal relationship between client exposure and compassion fatigue (Pearlman and MacIan 1995; Schauben and Frazier 1995; Jenkins and Baird 2002). The consequence of these conceptual and methodological problems has been contradictory results and the general finding that most professionals providing trauma therapy have little difficulty coping with the demands of their work (Sabin-Farrel and Turpin 2003). Conceptual clarity and more rigorous study designs, we think, can assist in identifying the professional caregivers most vulnerable to compassion fatigue and advance our understanding of the potential occupational and environmental hazards of this work.

To address these limitations, Boscarino and C.R.F. conducted the first comprehensive test of the concept of compassion fatigue by comparing social workers in the New York metro area who were or were not exposed to traumatized clients (Boscarino, Figley, and Adams 2004). Experience suggests that individuals working in the caring and psychotherapeutic professions are among those to provide mental health services to disaster victims suffering from psychological trauma following catastrophic events. Yet few studies have focused on the emotional exhaustion that comes from working with such clients, referred to as compassion fatigue, and how this differs from other occupational hazards, such as job burnout. In their 2004 study, Boscarino, Figley, and Adams used recently validated scales to predict compassion fatigue and job burnout related to providing services to those affected by the World Trade Center (WTC) attacks of 2001. The study data were based on a random survey of 236 social workers living in New York City, over 80 percent of whom reported being involved in post-WTC disaster counseling efforts. Their analyses indicated that, controlling for demographic factors, years of counseling, and personal trauma history, compassion fatigue was positively associated with WTC recovery involvement ($p < .001$) and negatively associated with having a supportive work environment ($p < .01$). In contrast, job burnout was negatively associated with having a supportive work environment ($p < .01$), but *not* associated with WTC involvement or WTC counseling efforts. The results support all major aspects of the original formulation of compassion fatigue (Figley 1995).

Traumatic Countertransference and Vicarious Trauma Responses

In addition to compassion fatigue and secondary traumatic stress reactions are two other closely related terms that we discuss briefly.

Countertransference to the traumatized. Although countertransference is linked to psychoanalytic theory and has been in the literature for many years (Neumann and Gamble 1995), it had limited use for understanding STS reactions among practitioners. The more contemporary perspective on countertransference involves the spontaneous or evoked responses of the therapist in regard to information provided, behaviors exhibited, and/or emotions displayed by the traumatized client. Danieli (1996) describes countertransference related to working with clients presenting massive traumatic experiences as traumatic, or event, countertransference:

> Countertransference reactions...inhibit professionals from studying, correctly diagnosing, and treating the effects of trauma. They also tend to perpetuate traditional training, which ignores the need for professionals to cope with massive real trauma and its long-term effects. (196)

One study (Hayes et al. 1991) identified characteristics that potentially manage the countertransference effects in the context of delivering psychothertherapy. Although not noted elsewhere, countertransference may play some role in the context of delivery services by animal-care workers. Hayes et al. found that self-integration, stress management, conceptualizing, empathy, and self-insight are associated with managing countertransference. Therefore, managing countertransference is seen more as a function of personality composition and is related to unresolved conflict within the therapist.

Caregivers working with survivors suffering from exposure to cruelty often experience reactions and find the cruelty fairly easy to visualize, thereby potentially keeping the provider from remaining engaged with the client. That is, as a way of defending themselves from hearing the client/survivor's traumatic material, providers may dissociate to some degree, distance themselves, question the veracity of the story being told, experience somatic responses, and be overwhelmed with feelings of grief or helplessness. If the traumatic experiences "touch" on any personal traumatic history, the therapist may become somewhat numb and not hear the client (Danieli 1996).

Whether confronting classical or traumatic countertransference, a therapist must possess a healthy character structure, be able to control anxiety, actively use conceptual skills, be able to maintain empathy while disengaged from the process of identification, and work on bringing unconscious material into conscious awareness to manage countertransference effectively (Hayes et al. 1991). Managing countertransference is essential because of the possibility of developing STS.

Vicarious trauma (VT). In the process of providing services to survivors, caregivers are exposed to traumatic material that begins to affect their world view, emotional and psychological needs, belief system, and cognitions, which develop over time. VT is a result of empathic engagement with survivors' trauma material (Pearlman and Saakvitne 1995; Schauben and Frazier 1995). It is recognized as normal, predictable, and inevitable, yet, if caregivers do not work with the transformation that is taking place, it can have a serious effect on them as individuals and as professionals. It can also affect interpersonal relationships (McCann and Pearlman 1990; Pearlman and Saakvitne 1995).

Janoff-Bulman (1989) discusses the fact that everyone has beliefs and assumptions, and these are often challenged when one experiences stressful life events, including a traumatic experience. The assumptions have also been identified as "schemas," as previously cited. The three basic assumptions include the perceived benevolence of the world, the meaningfulness of the world, and the worthiness of self. When a person is victimized or traumatized, these assumptions can be challenged.

VT can be addressed through acceptance and recognition of the changes that occur, through giving oneself permission to limit exposure to the pain of clients, and to expand one's knowledge about trauma generally and its direct and indirect effects on caregivers in particular. It is also important to be sensitive, when in the course of providing care to clients, to caregivers' feeling increased VT-related distress and why. Then one can use that information to better set limits with clients.

A study by Lee (1995) explored the development of STS from the perspective of compassion fatigue and VT. The purpose of the study was to determine the degree of STS among marriage and family therapists (MFTs) and the major factors that cause it. The study found that MFTs were often exposed to traumatized clients (63 percent of clients with a diagnosis of PTSD on average). It was not surprising that this group of MFTs scored higher levels of (secondary) traumatic stress than did medical students. Yet MFTs were found to experience little cognitive disruption. Indeed, MFTs' STS was directly related to their cognitive schemas and their level of satisfaction with their total caseload. Similarly, the more hours they were exposed to clients' traumatic material, the greater the MFTs' distress (e.g., intrusion scores).

Lee's research was consistent with an earlier study by Pearlman and MacIan (1995), which found that more experienced caregivers had fewer disruptions in self-trust than did those who are inexperienced. The difference was even greater when the inexperienced caregivers had little or no supervision.

Schauben and Frazier (1995) explored the effects on female mental health professionals of working with sexual assault survivors specific to STS from a perspective of VT and PTSD symptoms. They also explored the effects of therapists' victimization histories and their coping mechanisms for job-related stress. The results indicated that therapists with higher percentages of survivors in their caseload reported more cognitive schema disruptions, more VT, and more PTSD symptoms. The five most common coping mechanisms used were associated with lower levels of symptoms. Prior trauma history of the therapists and the interaction term were not significant.

Toward a Humane Workplace

Understanding the importance of a supportive work environment for preventing or helping to mitigate work-related distress, how can managers help? Let us look first at the signs of work-related distress among animal-care providers; at strategies for discussing and implementing a program of self-care, stress management, and instilling a sense of achievement; and at accentuating resilience and resiliency in the workplace.

Symptoms

The many signs of secondary stress or compassion fatigue among animal-care providers are listed in Table 3.1. It should be obvious in reviewing these symptoms that distress associated with dispensing compassion is pervasive and potentially long lasting. Later we talk about those who may feel that they are stuck. The first step in the process of confronting compassion stress and fatigue is a self-assessment. Indeed, the research on animal caregivers (see chapters 5 and 6) shows them experiencing considerable compassion fatigue, yet on average they love their jobs and derive considerable satisfaction from caring for animals.

Self-Assessments and Confronting the Problems

Once it is clear that something needs to be done beyond reducing or eliminating the emotionally toxic elements within the work environment, the time comes to manage one's responses effectively, both at work and away. Please refer to appendix A, where you will find the Academy of Traumatology's Standards of Self-Care, along with guidelines for following these standards.

The Need for Transformation for Those Who Are Stuck

"Stuck" is knowing that you have work-related distress, particularly compassion fatigue, but are unsure how and when to change. The Green Cross Foundation *(www.GreenCross.Org)* initiated a major program, The *You Too!* Wellness Weekend™, in 2005. Participants come together in a relaxed environment for three days to focus on themselves. Most are professionals and volunteers who work with the most challenging of clients and situations and who view their work as a "calling." Most have the tendency to help others and forget about themselves. These are the primary candidates for compassion fatigue.

The *You Too!* Wellness Weekend™ does far more than educate participants about burnout and the symptoms of STS. Participants learn about who is most vulnerable not only to job-related stress but also to themselves—not just professionally but personally, spiritually, interpersonally. Participants learn what they want for the rest of their lives; develop a plan for attaining it; and identify the people, places, and things (real and imagined) that are blocking them from realizing their hopes and dreams.

Some of these things are associated with specific skills and knowledge (e.g., stress management, spirituality, intuition-development, and self-healing) learned during the weekend. These features emerge directly from the research literature in self-improvement and career development because that is what so many in the caring field need now. This is why the Green Cross Foundation has focused so much energy and so many resources on this project.

The most challenging part of the the *You Too!* Wellness Weekend™ is enabling participants to make changes in their lives. Similar to keeping New Year's resolutions, the intent is there—what is lacking is follow-through. This is where the Green Cross Foundation's MASTERS Process of Wellness Transformation helps to insure follow through. The process requires, for example, adopting the right attitude toward wellness in our lives, starting with the intention to change parts and patterns of our lives. The process is challenging but well worth the effort, because in the end the participants' lives are happier, healthier, and more productive. From more than two decades of research in human resources, change-required commitment, analysis, planning, and experimentation, the MASTERS Process of Wellness Transformation provides a description of (or prescription for) seven building blocks for life transformation. It is not easy, it is not based on faith or social support or anything other than a total commitment on the part of the participants to first recognize that they have neglected themselves for too long and, as a result, have neglected those they love and serve as well. Here then are the seven building blocks as related to our participants at the foundation's *You Too!* Wellness Weekend™.

> Everyone has beliefs and assumptions, and these are often challenged when one experiences stressful life events.

Building Block One: Motivation. Intention is setting your mind to a particular task; motivation is the force needed to actually carry out the task. People make New Year's resolutions with every good intention, but without adequate energy and action, they never even *try* to fulfill their intention. Motivation is required, not only to set goals for a life plan for wellness, but also to establish a workable plan, carry it out, and fine-tune it to actually acquire wellness at the most appropriate level, a level that is at the lowest level or highest level depending upon the resources of the person seeking wellness, such as the time or money available. The MASTERS Process of Wellness Transformation will never be completed unless there is sufficient motivation throughout the process. Thus, we define *motivation* in the Process of Wellness Transformation as the intention, commitment, energy, and sustenance to complete transformation to the most appropriate level.

Building Block Two: Assessment. Assessment requires motivation. It is completing a battery of tests and procedures that result in additional information about how we are functioning with regard to stress, coping, and social support. It also includes efforts to discover our hopes and dreams about future functioning. Assessment in some ways is a mirror, providing images of our psychosocial and emotional functioning that, when observed, reveal where improvements are needed.

Thus, we define assessment in the process of wellness transformation as *the gathering of factual and objective information that informs us from where we are now to where we want to be and which may lead to a healthier and happier self.*

Building Block Three: Self-reflection. The next building block in the transformation process toward wellness is self-reflection. Self-reflection begins after the process of assessment and involves careful consideration of what this information represents to the person in his or her journey toward transformation. Self-reflection requires honesty, concentration, and vision. This building block is critical in fairly interpreting the self-assessment, and not only in identifying the areas that require change and development. Self-reflection requires recognizing and retaining one's strengths, satisfactions, and sustenance throughout the transformative process and for the rest of one's life. Too often we ignore or do not appreciate our positive features—our kindness, compassion, sensitivity, civility, humor—and become transfixed by what we are missing and want to acquire. C.R.F. defines self-reflection in the process of wellness transformation as the process of taking stock of what to keep and what to change to ensure lifelong wellness.

Building Block Four: Transformation. One of the most important building blocks, transformation reflections lead to constructing the first draft of a life plan for wellness and transformation for the rest of one's life. It is a process by which we make explicit what we perceived in the assessment results and considered in the self-reflection process. It is transforming information and insight into a solid, measurable, usable wellness life plan. We define a person's life plan as a never-ending, always evolving set of standards and activities that assure wellness for him or her. We define *wellness transformation* as a process of shifting from one mind-set that lacks wellness to one that embraces and moves toward wellness. We define *transformation reflection* as the process by which we concentrate on what we need to acquire and retain wellness in contrast to where we are at the time, and we do this reflecting in a state of peace and calm (i.e., being centered) rather than under duress or in distress.

Building Block Five: Evaluating. The fifth building block in the MASTERS Process of Wellness Transformation is *evaluation*, the process of seeking, finding, and learning about those life skills that are tools for achieving our life plan for wellness. Life skills for wellness are defined as those skills that help us become and remain healthy and happy and in a constant state of wellness. These life skills include but are not limited to our ability to select and/or consume the right (1) physical activities, (2) nutrition, (3) stress management and desensitization, (4) spirituality, (5) sense of humor, (6) self-awareness, and (7) other resources, skills, and techniques to acquire and retain wellness. We define evaluating for wellness as *the process of learning about the life skills necessary for acquiring and retaining wellness, learning these skills, and practicing them on a regular basis.*

Building Block Six: Reviewing. Reviewing for wellness includes two review processes following acquisition and practice of the necessary life skills. The first review involves reviewing one's life up to the present. It involves identifying major life achievements and catastrophes and considering when they happened, why they happened, and what one learned from the experience at the time and at present. The second review process involves reviewing and (if needed) revising the current draft of one's life plan for wellness, in light of newly acquired skills and the results of the life review. We define reviewing for wellness and transformation as the *dual process of learning from the past with newly acquired life skills and formulating the best life plan to complete and retain the transformative process.*

Building Block Seven: Studying. The final building block of the MASTERS Process of Wellness Transformation is studying, which begins when the wellness life plan is implemented. Rarely are plans perfect, and most often they require some adjustments. What one studies is how the life plan is working and whether any obvious adjustments are required to make it work better. The longer one lives with the life plan for wellness, the fewer changes and adjustments are necessary. In the first year, however, studying the life plan leads to many, many changes and adjustments for peak wellness. We define studying the wellness plan as *the process of carefully measuring the benefits and costs of each element of the plan.* Using such an analysis will help the person make improvements to the plan to insure that it is useful long into the future.

Humane Society University's Approach

The mission of The Humane Society of the United States (HSUS) is to create a humane and sustainable world for all animals, including people. Through education, public policy advocacy, and the promotion of best practices in all facets and at all levels of animal welfare work, it seeks to forge lasting and comprehensive changes in attitude and behavior; relieve animal suffering; prevent abuse and neglect; and protect wild animals and their environments.

Humane Society University (HSU) is an essential component of The HSUS's commitment to the promotion of professional practices within the animal-control and -sheltering community. Animal-care and animal-control personnel, wildlife rehabilitators, and animal organization volunteers and board members are HSU's primary constituencies. This makes HSU virtually unique as a corporate university whose target audiences consist of individuals associated with a range of independent groups not affiliated with its parent organization.

HSU began to incorporate courses and seminars on professional leadership development to help animal-care and -control personnel gain the skills and knowledge necessary for job success and career advancement. Through HSU The HSUS has moved toward a comprehensive strategy for promoting professionalization and its corollary benefits, meeting a long apparent need for advanced training.

Background and survey research concerning the needs of the field directly influence HSU's emphasis on courses on social marketing, compassion fatigue, humane education, and the relationship between cruelty to animals and interpersonal violence. These concerns are central to animal protection work.

From the perspective of the animal-care and animal-control field, in which funding for training is extremely limited, distance learning is an especially promising development. It eliminates time, inconvenience, and expenses associated with travel and accommodations, and permits employees to pursue coursework without having to abandon their daily responsibilities.

The intensity of work-related stress among animal-shelter employees has created a heavy demand for compassion fatigue workshops—which acknowledge and attempt to address the impact of high-pressure responsibilities on shelter personnel. Animal caregivers are among the most susceptible to compassion fatigue because of the toll that performing euthanasia takes on their psyche. Unlike other caregivers, animal caregivers do not have patients who can verbally express their pain and suffering; they instead must rely on their own experience to make decisions for their patients. This phenomenon, the so-called care-killing paradox, is discussed in HSU-sponsored workshops, as is how to recognize the signs of compassion fatigue, how the signs affect individuals and their employers, and, finally, how to manage the signs themselves. These day-long workshops detail the history of compassion fatigue, how to distinguish compassion fatigue from other daily life stresses, and the typical symptoms of compassion fatigue. Students complete a self-test (appendix B) and score the test to determine their risk for compassion fatigue.

> Animal caregivers are among the most susceptible to compassion fatigue because of the toll that performing euthanasia takes.

During the workshops students learn to develop coping strategies that will focus their energies on alleviating their symptoms. Students learn techniques to alter the stresses in their lives and why the need exists to develop a balanced lifestyle. In-class exercises help students understand how a balanced lifestyle will help alleviate compassion fatigue. The focus of the exercises is typically career, money, health, family, and friends, among other topics. At the end of the course, individualized action plans are developed that will help students to increase the level of satisfaction they experience in each of the above areas.

Most important in HSU's recent planning has been the introduction of an enhanced online component, especially in management, humane education, and anti-cruelty law enforcement training. The HSUS has made a strong commitment to online education, purchasing a superior learning platform, recruiting new course developers and instructors, forging new strategic partnerships, and increasing its marketing of online training programs.

Conclusion

I t is not easy to change, and life change is often reactive rather than proactive. That is, most of us change as a result of a catastrophe—the death of a loved one, ill health, an accident, or other calamity. Changing often requires the help of others—friends, colleagues, or professionals we pay for their services. Some people have little difficulty seeking help. Others find it nearly impossible. Still others for various reasons rarely consider that they need help. Yet the *You Too!* Wellness Weekend™ transformation requires some form of reaching out and securing help. There are some stumbling blocks to transformation, including what C.R.F. has described as the stress-coping personalities. C.R.F. defines them as *a set of traits and characteristics associated with the way stress is perceived and managed, with special attention to the way people seek, secure, and use help.* Change is never easy; you need a plan. We believe that, more than any other education and training, those who work with the traumatized first need to turn inward and examine if and how things need to change and develop a strategy for doing so—for the benefit of everyone.

The Bond

CHAPTER

For compassion fatigue to occur, a caregiving relationship must exist. The nature of this relationship must include a caregiver and one or more clients. The relationship must also include the exchange of empathy, emotions, and information between the caregiver and the client. There must be a strong desire on the part of the caregiver to help alleviate the suffering and pain of the client. In the absence of these variables, compassion fatigue will not occur. And, as a practical matter, no client improvement will occur. Those in the animal-care profession always have multiple clients—animals (owned or otherwise), the owners of the animals, and other involved humans. At the core of all of our work in the animal-care profession is the relationship that exists between us as helpers and the animals themselves. In the animal-care profession, this relationship is called the human-animal bond.

Veterinarians Stanley Diesch, R.K. Anderson, and William McCulloch and psychiatrist David McCulloch coined the term in 1977 (American Veterinary Medical Association 1998), following a 1975 study commissioned by the National Institutes of Health documenting "The Human Health Responsibilities of Veterinarians." This study was the first official recognition of the triangular relationship among people, their veterinarians, and their pets (American Veterinary Medical Association 1998).

The concept and dynamic of the human-animal bond were first tested legally in a 1979 lawsuit (*Corso vs. Crawford Dog and Cat Hospital*. 415 N.Y.S. 2d 182 [1979]) in which a pet owner claimed "emotional distress" when an animal hospital switched the cremated remains of her pet with those of another. The court awarded the claimant $700. More important than the award, however, was that the courts established a national precedent, recognizing and giving value to the human-animal bond.

To fully understand the human-animal bond, key terms should be defined. These key terms are:

- *Bond*—"A thing or force that unites or restrains. A binding agreement. To hold or tie together. To connect or reinforce" *(The Oxford Dictionary).*
- *Relationship*—"The state or instance of being related, connected, or associated. The emotions associated between two people or entities" *(The Oxford Dictionary).*

The human-animal bond is defined as

[A] mutually beneficial and dynamic relationship between people and other animals that is influenced by behaviors that are essential to the health and well being of both. This includes but is not limited to emotions, psychological and physical interactions of people, other animals, and the environment. (American Veterinary Medical Association 1998, n.p.)

During early discussions about the human-animal bond, much of the writing reflected anecdotal or case presentations. Then, in 1987 the National Institutes of Health (NIH) held a landmark technological assessment workshop examining the health benefits of human-animal interaction. The NIH recommended that further interdisciplinary, collaborative research look critically at the relationship among companion animals, people, and medicine (American Veterinary Medical Association 1998). This event was a milestone, marking the transition of the human-animal bond from a qualitative to a quantitative field.

Research into the human-animal bond as of 2005 was firmly rooted in science. In 2002 PAWSitive Inter Action published its research findings in a paper, entitled "A Scientific Look at the Human-Animal Bond" (PAWSitive Inter Action 2002). The authors were:

- *Alan Beck,* Sc. D., director of the Center for the Human-Animal Bond at the School of Veterinary Medicine, Purdue University

- *Sandra Barker,* Ph.D., professor of psychiatry and director of the Center for Human-Animal Interaction, School of Medicine, Virginia Commonwealth University
- *Marty Becker,* D.V.M., author of *The Healing Power of Pets*
- *Edward Cresgam,* M.D., professor, the Mayo Clinic Medical School, American Cancer Society, professor of clinical oncology and The John and Roma Rouse professor of humanism in medicine.

> For compassion fatigue to occur, a caregiving relationship must exist.

Following the 1987 recommendations, PAWSitive Inter Action concluded that "science has officially weighed in on the human-animal bond and the evidence is clear. Research demonstrates that human-animal interaction benefits physical, emotional and psychological wellness" (PAWSitive Inter Action 2002, 9).

This study was limited to findings within the United States, but a more global view and understanding of the information was needed. In 2003 that information was provided by Bonnie Beaver, D.V.M. According to Beaver, "People throughout the world relate to animals on the basis of such factors as their society, culture, and personal values" (2003, 1). She adds that, in more developed countries, the human-animal bond is stronger as a result of basic human needs having been met and the existence of more disposable income to provide for animals (Beaver 2003).

As in any emotional relationship, the human-animal bond has both positive and negative aspects. How do we express the positive side of the human-animal bond? Seventy-eight percent of pet owners report that their pets greet them when they come home from work, but their spouses do not (Fucco 2002). Ninety-seven percent of pet owners report that their pets make them smile at least once a day; 76 percent believe that pets reduce stress; and 85 percent report that their pets show concern when they are sick (Fucco 2002).

The human-animal bond is not related to age. PAWsitive Inter Action concluded that

> In an era of concern about the soaring price of medical care, the profit of the benefits of the human-animal bond has important implications for controlling costs and improving health in a growing population of senior

citizens. Indeed, policies that encourage pet ownership among the aged, either at home or as they make the transition to elder living facilities, can absolutely improve some medical conditions and alleviate loneliness. (2003, 9)

A. Arluke (in Winiarskyj 2001) posits that children ages eleven to sixteen can be "animal people." Young people who have a strong self-image see relationships with animals as being reciprocal. The children reported "getting something back" for helping animals. Winiarskyj (2001) reported that children regularly exposed to animals have more empathy for animals than do those without such exposure.

Most of the research on the human-animal bond focuses on the positive aspect of the relationship; however, some reports focus on the negative side the relationship. The Vermont Veterinary Medical Association [n.d., n.p.] reports:

You cannot just tie a dog to the dog house, throw it a bone and expect bonding to occur. At the other extreme, people who treat their pets as surrogate children and overindulge their pet can produce a behavioral problem that is hard to control...Another side effect of the bond is the grief many people feel when they part with their pet. In preparing an answer for you, I consulted an animal behavior modification specialist. He noted that children's grief is a special concern particularly when a pet must be euthanized or removed from the home...The relationship can be extremely beneficial but it can have problematic side effects. Most of us are willing to put up with some inconveniences. We also should be alert for serious problems that need correcting...

When the human-animal bond is broken by animal abuse, neglect, or torture, it is no wonder that those of us who are caregivers are moved to our own personal anger toward the perpetrator. Our anger gives way to our desire to help the suffering animal(s). It is this desire to help that leads us down the road of compassion fatigue.

We will examine various positions within the animal-care profession in an effort to understand compassion fatigue.

The Animal-Shelter Environment

Kim Intino, manager of the Animal Services Consultation (ASC) of The HSUS, confirms that there is no industry-wide definition of an animal shelter. The ASC program uses the following criteria in its definition (personal communication with R.G.R., November 1, 2005):
- A regular 501(c)(3) nonprofit organization
- An organization that operates an animal-shelter facility at a fixed address and maintains it primarily for the purpose of sheltering animals
- One that handles about a hundred companion animals a year
- One that maintains regular visiting hours for the general public

Using the aforementioned definition, most shelter organizational charts resemble the structure seen in Figure 5.1.

Why People Choose to Work at a Shelter

Many people enter the animal-care profession because they want to help animals; however, most are not completely cognizant of the emotional demands and/or consequences of their chosen profession (White 1998).

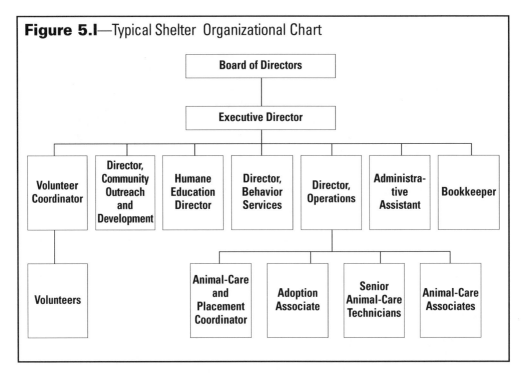

Figure 5.1—Typical Shelter Organizational Chart

Wagner (2000) lists many reasons why people enter the profession, including:

- A love of animals (this is the predominant response given at every compassion fatigue workshop led by R.G.R.)
- Care and compassion for animals and people
- A purpose in life/sense of calling
- A desire to do something worthwhile with one's life
- A sense of enjoyment from working with animals
- A desire to play and/or be with animals
- A desire to help/be part of the solution
- A concern for the welfare of animals
- A desire to give animals a better way of life
- A desire to alleviate suffering
- A desire to find good homes for animals
- It is important work

Overwhelmingly, one can conclude from White (1998) and Wagner (2000) that people are drawn to work in shelters because of a strong desire to be a caregiver to animals.

If the reasons that draw people to their work are noble and theoretically lead people to rewarding careers, then why are so many animal caregivers so unhappy? This is an extremely complex question, and the answer lies in the reasons for engaging in the work initially. As with many professions or positions, stress or pressure comes not only from the nature of the work, but from internal and external sources as well. In addition, many shelter positions give way to an emotional commitment since the workers form relationships with animals, people, and co-workers. Subsequently, these factors will affect the formation and framework of the shelter worker's self-value and self-esteem.

In 1988 Rick Collord, executive director, Humane Society of Broward County (1988) organized euthanasia workshops for employees of humane societies. Because he was sensitized to the trauma of compassion fatigue, he arranged for a hospice care bereavement specialist to conduct the sessions. The problem as described by the specialist was that euthanasia workers have difficulty working through the normal grieving process because animal deaths are so prevalent and never ending. Collord concluded that shelter workers' inability to handle the trauma of euthanasia led to feelings of isolation and low self-esteem and, as a result, complicated their work relationships. Current research demonstrates that stress and compassion fatigue are found in workers throughout shelters and are not limited only to those performing euthanasia (HSUS 2003–2004).

These resulting emotions can serve as the framework for how animal-care professionals deal with the day-to-day activities of their jobs. A compassion fatigue survey administered to animal-care workers revealed that, despite great suffering, personal pain, and witness to animal suffering, they continue in the profession because of their passion for it. This mind-set develops into a form of emotional self-injury.

This emotional self-injury is comparable in nature to the dynamic of physical self-injury. In physical self-injury, inner emotions and pain are expressed as external pain. This self-injury is an overt expression of the pain. In emotional self-injury, the pain remains internalized.

In addition to the emotional nature of the work, animal-care professionals experience significant external and internal pressures that affect the conditions in which they must work. The external stresses that shelter workers face include:

- Public perception and lack of understanding
- Relationships with other humans and animals

- Friends and family who do not understand the work
- Government regulation and administrators
- Negative media
- Requests for special favors from politicians and friends

These examples suggest that external stressors, especially how the public reacts to the work, contribute greatly to the nature of the work at the shelter and no doubt demonstrate that the toll the public inflicts on a shelter worker is profound. "Shelter workers do the dirty work for the general population members who continue to breed, abuse, overpopulate animals, and shift the blame onto shelter staff for a problem they created themselves" (Wagner 2000, 1).

Internal pressures must be considered as well, as these can have a great impact on the emotions of animal-shelter workers. Some examples of these pressures include:

- Staffing levels
- Volume of animals
- Hours of operation
- Adoption rates
- Financial health of the shelter
- Nature of the work
- Mentality of indispensability
- Board of directors
- Relationships with co-workers

Is the work worth it? Wagner (2000) has assembled the most comprehensive list of rewards inherent to working in a shelter. They consist of:

- Loving the animals
- Happy endings and success stories associated with finding homes for the animals
- Being part of the solution and having a positive impact on animals' lives and pet owners' perceptions
- Reuniting animals with owners
- Facilitating adoption and making good matches
- Seeing an animal placed in a lasting, loving home
- Seeing animals leave with responsible new owners
- Adoption of hard-to-place animals
- Hearing back from those who have adopted
- Rescuing strays before they are injured

While shelter workers report liking or even loving their work, they often say that what they do is for others. There are numerous reports of animal-care workers hearing, "I couldn't do what you do," or "I love animals too much to do your work." As a result of such comments, which animal-shelter workers perceive as hurtful, workers may say, "I work for the government," or "I work for a nonprofit," rather than divulging their precise employer. However, such lack of candor truly hurts shelter workers' self-esteem and self-value; consequently, animal-care workers have reported developing a dislike of humans.

This detachment from others only seems to strengthen isolation and reduce self-esteem. When removing the isolation and reducing the stress, the evidence indicates that self-esteem cannot be raised (Braun 1996). With all of this rejection and pain, the question that begs to be asked is: "What price do animal caregivers pay?" Workers report statements such as (White 1998):

- "I hate myself for being part of it."
- "I have a lot of sleepless nights."
- "I entered therapy in the beginning of June and am being medicated for severe depression."
- "I do not get too personally involved, so I can't say that it hurts me."
- "I have been here long enough to know not to get attached to the animals, but sometimes I still do."

Smith (1990, 5-5) reported shelter and animal-control employee comments such as:

- "Sometimes my anger pounds the air."
- "I wish I could reach out to all of those who have to deal with this pain and give them a big hug and take some of that pain away."
- "We are dog lovers, yet [we are] the ones who suffer."
- "I feel that I am here to do the dirty work and that makes me angry."
- "My feelings are hate because people think I have no feelings. Wanting to quit, but I cannot because what if no one else cares."
- "The anger is usually directed, if only mentally, at the pet owner, some technicians displace their anger and it invades their personal life."

W.H. Smith (1990) conducted seminars, entitled "Euthanasia: The Human Factor," for The HSUS in the 1980s and early '90s. He was one of the original observers to record symptoms of animal-shelter and animal-control workers. Smith says these feelings of guilt and anger "are complex," yet calls them "a problem with no name." In light of what is known today, Smith was observing classic symptoms of compassion fatigue; the "problem with no name" Smith observed in 1980 was compassion fatigue.

People continue in the field because they love their work; however, this love causes them terrible pain. These feelings and reactions have not changed in more than twenty-five years.

> People continue in the field because they love their work; this love causes them terrible pain.

As validated by current data collection and earlier reporting, there is little doubt that compassion fatigue is pervasive in animal shelters and the animal-control community. We must also make room for the possibility that compassion fatigue in the animal-care community is a by-product of multiple high-risk exposures. These exposures are thought to be high risk because animal-care workers are exposed to them constantly and repeatedly. This, in turn, increases the compassion fatigue. Examples of high-risk exposure include:

- Public perception that the work is low level and "not noble"
- Budget cuts
- Physical environment: space, noise, and lighting
- Co-workers
- Volume of animals

Perhaps the most prevalent high-risk factor in animal shelters is the sheer number of animals entering the facilities. The volume of animals produces an almost impossible level of work and, accordingly, leads to unattainable goals. Let us compare a social worker or counselor, who may spend one hour per patient, working five days a week for six hours a day, and see thirty patients a week. The animal-care professional "sees" *hundreds* of "cases" per week. Some of these cases—lost animals reunited with their owners, injured animals made well and placed for adoption—end happily and productively. However, many (in some cases, the majority) of these cases are resolved by destruction of the "patient," via euthanasia, even after days or weeks of effort by the workers themselves.

The employee skill level, the desire to help the animals, and self-isolation place the animal-care professional in an "at-risk" population. This "at-risk" label is supported by Holland's theory of "a personality-occupation typology." In this hypothesis, Holland (in Antony 1998) developed a personality-based theory of occupational choices that was guided by two assumptions—that occupational choices are a reflection of personality and that descriptions of occupational interest provide insight into one personality. Holland developed six basic personality types: realistic, investigative, artistic, social, enterprising, and conventional. The realistic type is defined as one who "prefers activities involving the manipulation of machinery, tools, or animals and may lack social skills." The lack of socials skills adds to the worker's isolation.

Tillett (2003) cites Malan and discusses "a helping profession syndrome," in which an individual chooses (usually unconsciously) to work as a caregiver as a response to the personal vulnerability of the patient within. Many professionals have a special relationship with their work; caregivers perceive the needs of others as greater than their own. This leads to caregivers as "self-sacrificers." If these attempts at caregiving are unsuccessful, caregivers become vulnerable to depression. Jacobs (1991) describes a "constructive vengeance," suggesting that caregivers are motivated by a desire to right perceived wrongs of the past, sublimating a wish for revenge into a conscious wish for reparation. Their giving of care to others in such a vigorous manner leads to severe physical fatigue and emotional exhaustion.

To best determine what is happening emotionally to the animal-care professional, the differential diagnosis approach is most helpful. In the practice of medicine, the differential diagnosis is a "dynamic process used to determine the disease suggested by the symptoms the patient is presenting, listing the most likely causes and using appropriate testing to include or exclude some of the possible causes" (Wikipedia n.d., n.p.). In using this approach, many different inputs are considered to reach an informed opinion. In administering the compassion fatigue scale to more than one thousand shelter workers and caregivers, several trends have emerged. R.G.R. (in The Humane Society of the United States 2003–2004) has termed these trends. They are:

- Compassion fatigue is not related to length of service.
- Compassion fatigue is not related to age.
- Compassion fatigue is only slightly related to gender, with females scoring higher than males.
- Compassion fatigue is not related to performing euthanasia.

In administering the CF self-test, one can observe that compassion fatigue is pronounced and widespread throughout the animal-care

Table 5.2—Compassion Fatigue Self-Test*

Score	Risk Level	Percent Self-Reporting
41 or above	Extremely high risk	56.4
36–40	High risk	11.7
31–35	Moderate risk	10.5
27–30	Low risk	7.3
26 or below	Extremely low risk	14.1

*Administered to 1,000 shelter and animal-control workers, 2003–2004.
Source: HSUS 2003–2004.

profession. In the shelter the positions of humane educator, executive director, kennel attendant, veterinarian, volunteer, operations manager, humane investigator, bookkeeper, adoption counselor, fundraiser, etc., in addition to euthanasia technician, are at equal risk of CF.

Research on compassion fatigue in many helping professions reveals that workers in shelters and animal control are at higher risk for compassion fatigue than are other caregivers.

Using the differential diagnosis and literature models, the following trends appear to occur for shelter and animal-care professionals:

- Animal-care professionals are caregivers.
- Animal caregivers have a higher "client load" than do human caregivers.
- Animal caregivers enter the profession because they love animals.
- Animal caregivers are subject to ongoing exposure to trauma and suffering.
- Animal caregivers may suffer feelings of isolation.
- Animal caregivers report developing a dislike of humans.
- Despite high trauma and compassion fatigue, animal caregivers stay in the job because they worry no one can replace them in caring for the animals.

Clearly, shelter and animal-care workers need assistance or resources to enable them to deal with compassion fatigue.

At the other end of the caregivers' emotional continuum is compassion satisfaction (CS). Stamm (2002, 112) defines CS as the sentiment arising from one who "derives pleasures from helping, likes colleagues, and feels good about [his or her] ability to help and making contributions."

In view of the rewards of working in a shelter (Wagner 2000), it is clear that compassion satisfaction and compassion fatigue exist within the shelter community. One of the authors (R.G.R., in The Humane Society of the United States 2003–2004) found the rates of compassion satisfaction described in Table 5.3.

When CF scores are compared to CS scores for the same individuals, 68.2 percent have good or better potential for CS, and within the same sample, 68.1 percent are at high or extremely high risk for CF. How can we reconcile this? How can one like what he or she does and continue to do it, even if it causes great pain? Stamm (2002, 113) examined these questions:

> One of the most intriguing questions raised by this line of inquiry is whether a person could be at high risk for experiencing CF and at the same time still experience high CS. At this point the hypothesis is that there is balance between the two. For example, from discussion with caregivers in various humanitarian settings, we came to understand that they believe they have CF, but many of

Table 5.3—Compassion Satisfaction Self-Test*

Score	Risk Level	Percent Self-Reporting
118 or above	Extremely high	3.4
100–117	High	22.1
82–99	Good potential	42.7
64–81	Modest potential	21.7
63 or below	Low potential	9.5

*Administered to 1,000 shelter and animal-control workers.
Source: HSUS 2003–2004.

Table 5.4—Burnout Self-Test*

Score	Risk Level	Percent Self-Reporting
76–85	Extremely high risk	0.9
51–75	High	17.8
31–50	Moderate risk	34.9
36 or below	Extremely low risk	46.3

*Administered to 1,000 shelter and animal-control workers.
Source: HSUS 2003–2004.

them like their work because they feel positive benefits from it. They believe what they are doing is helping a group of people and in some ways that it is even redemptive. Certainly they believe it is the right thing to do.

While this research and these finding focused on individuals providing care to humans, their ramifications also translate to those providing care to animals.

In addition to CF and CS, shelter and animal-control workers are subject to burnout: "the state of physical and emotional and mental exhaustion caused by the depletion of ability to cope with one's environment resulting from our responses to the ongoing demand characteristics (stress) of our daily lives" (Maslach 1982, 11). This definition implies that burnout is a result of stress. Valent (2002) concluded that burnout is the result of an inability to accomplish work goals. Given the great number of animals with whom shelter workers and animal-control professionals must deal—depending on the size of the shelter, it is likely to deal with several thousand animals—it is very likely that there is a feeling of not being able to accomplish work objectives.

It is not surprising that 53.6 percent of the surveyed shelter workers and animal-control professionals are at high or moderate risk of burnout (Table 5.4). These are undoubtedly professions that make very high emotional demands of their workers. Using the differential diagnosis model, the need to recognize and deal with combinations of CF, CS, and burnout (BO) is ever present.

The Practice of Veterinary Medicine and Compassion Fatigue

6

CHAPTER

Fast Facts

- Compassion fatigue, burnout, and compassion satisfaction are not significantly different for male and female veterinary professionals.
- Compassion fatigue, burnout, and compassion satisfaction scores of those who are involved in performing euthanasia are not significantly different from scores of those who are not involved in euthanasia.
- Scores for all members of veterinary practice teams are similar, although veterinarians and office staff identified different sources of stress and satisfaction.
- Healing animals and the opportunity to work as a team are major sources of satisfaction for all staff.

As we all know, people love their pets. When our pets need health care, we turn to veterinarians for treatment. In a "normal day," a veterinarian deals with a wide range of medical conditions. A range of literature discusses CF and veterinarians. Mitchener and Ogilvie (2002) asked the question, "Do I care too much?" and go on to discuss in some broad detail how to "self-treat" oneself for compassion fatigue. Manette (2004) wrote a commentary in *The Journal of American Veterinary Medicine* that was mainly philosophic in nature. "The Weight of Compassion" (Vogel 2004) portrays a conversation between a veterinarian and a clinical social worker. After listening to the veterinarian for a few minutes, the social worker concludes that the veterinarian has CF.

While it is clear that veterinarians and staff members are caregivers, there is no quantifiable study of CF within the small-animal (as opposed to large-animal, or livestock) practice office setting.

The veterinary practice is unique due to the role imposed on the veterinarian. Crimi (1998) cites an American Animal Hospital Association report in which 70 percent of pet owners described their pets as children. These clients expect veterinarians to act more like pediatricians in their doctor-client relationships. This role confusion on the part of the client contributes to the stress level in the relationship. If the client does not understand the correct role of the veterinarian, then the client's behavior is likely to be inappropriate and the source of heightened emotions, especially during medical/health crises. By extension, the same dynamic would occur for all staff throughout the practice setting, including the receptionist, animal-health technician, kennel worker, bookkeeper, etc. Different positions in the practice setting have different stressors and different degrees of compassion fatigue.

The scant literature on compassion fatigue within the veterinarian practice focuses on the veterinarian and does not address the office staff. To learn more about CF, CS, and BO within the veterinarian practice, R.G.R. (in The Humane Society of the United States 2003–2004) administered the Compassion Satisfaction and Fatigue survey to veterinarians, veterinary techs, veterinary assistants, and office staff in more than two hundred practices. These individuals were asked to list the top three stressors and top three on-the-job satisfiers. R.G.R. presented the results of this survey at the 2004 American Animal Hospital Association annual meeting. Table 6.1 represents the findings of CF in veterinarians.

Based on these data, one-third of veterinarians are at high or extremely high risk for CF. While this risk exposure is lower than that of animal-shelter workers and animal-control professionals, it is obvious that working as an animal caregiver leads to CF.

To learn more about stress on veterinarians, the survey asked them to list their top three sources of stress. The results are presented in Table 6.2.

Two of the top three stressors for veterinarians include interaction with clients; interaction with animals was not listed. In light of Crimi's comments, we need to be ask why clients can act in such a difficult manner with their "surrogate pediatrician." If people were more appreciative, the work setting would be a more emotionally satisfying environment. One could come to the conclusion that veterinarians need to establish the most efficient way for members of their practice to deal with difficult people.

The compassion satisfaction of veterinarians is directly related to animal care. The ability to help the patient is all-important to the practitioner. The survey asks veterinarians to list their top three items of job satisfaction. The compassion satisfaction of veterinarians is presented in Table 6.3.

The survey reveals that 82.7 percent of veterinarians show "good" or higher levels of potential for CS. While no studies measure CF or

Table 6.1—Compassion Fatigue and Veterinarians

Score	Risk Level	Percent Self-Reporting
41 or above	Extremely high risk	23.9
36–40	High risk	6.5
31–35	Moderate risk	23.9
27–30	Low risk	8.7
26 or below	Extremely low risk	37.0

Mail survey of 200 veterinarians' practices.
Source: HSUS 2003–2004.

Table 6.2—External Stressors and Veterinarians

Stressor	Percent Reporting
Difficult or noncompliant clients*	50.0
Not enough time	35.0
Discussing/disputing fees	35.0
Problems with staff performance	31.0
Concern about skills/accuracy	20.0
Lack of sufficient trained staff	15.0
Problems with co-workers	15.0
Others (e.g., noise, computer problems)	13.0

* The client was defined as the person who presents the animal. The patient is the animal.
Mail survey of 200 veterinarians' practices. (Multiple answers could be chosen.)
Source: HSUS 2003–2004.

Table 6.3—Compassion Satisfaction and Veterinarians

Score	Risk Level	Percent Self-Reporting
118 or above	Extremely high potential	8.7
100–117	High potential	37.0
82–99	Good potential	37.0
64–81	Modest potential	13.0
63 or below	Low potential	4.3

Mail survey of 200 veterinarians' practices.
Source: HSUS 2003–2004.

Table 6.4—Sources of Compassion Satisfaction

Source of Satisfaction	Percent Reporting
Helping/healing animals	81.3
Thankful clients	68.8
Working as a team	41.7
Using skills/learning new ones	29.2
Daily contact with animals	20.8
Educating clients	16.7
Financial rewards	12.5

Mail survey of 200 veterinarians' practices. (Multiple answers could be chosen.)
Source: HSUS 2003–2004.

CS across a wide range of medical specialties, this high percentage is encouraging. A closer review of specific items of job satisfaction presents a paradox for the veterinarian and the client relationship. Table 6.4 lists the top seven items that drive CS.

In reviewing veterinarians' stressors, interaction with difficult clients has the most negative effect. The paradox in the client relationship is that positive interaction with "thankful clients" is as powerful as negative interaction. However, the top item in CS is helping animals (81.3 percent). Hypothetically, does this mean that if the practice could be limited to appreciative clients, the veterinarian would have the perfect profession? However attractive that concept may be, the reality is clearly different. Comparison of the stressors and satisfiers confirms the need to deal effectively with both difficult and appreciative clients.

Veterinarians present the same dynamic of high CF and CS as do shelter and animal-control professionals. These high scores in CF and CS with low BO are termed bookend scores. These bookend scores demonstrate the need to increase the level of job satisfaction and bring more balance into veterinarians' lives. The lack of balance leads to more negative consequences than positive ones. Bookend scorers' single most important action is to increase CS. We are cautioned by Luechefeld (2005, 10–11): "The toughest decision comes when veterinarians feel forced to choose between the profession they love and spending time with the people they love."

The consequences of lack of balance have been noted: "Some veterinarians might find themselves dealing with health problems or addictions, including gambling, smoking and alcohol. Others might have problems sleeping or could find themselves making mistakes at work" (in Soares 2005, 11); and "His marriage, his health, everything had fallen out of balance. And for the most part, he realized the problems were self-inflicted"(Luechefeld 2005, 11).

Table 6.5—Burnout in Veterinarians

Score	Risk Level	Percent Self-Reporting
76–85	Extremely high risk	0
51–75	High risk	8.7
37–50	Moderate risk	32.6
0–36	Extremely low risk	58.7

Mail survey of 200 veterinarians' practices.
Source: HSUS 2003–2004.

When examining burnout in veterinarians, the picture is very positive, and the low scores in Table 6.5 complete the bookend picture. Stamm points out,

> Most people have an intuitive idea of what burnout is. From the research perspective, burnout is associated with feelings of hopelessness and difficulties in dealing with work or in doing your job effectively. These negative feelings usually have a gradual onset. They can reflect the feeling that your efforts make no difference, or they can be associated with a very high workload or a non-supportive work environment. (2005, 5)

The burnout scores reveal that veterinarians are in control when it comes to achieving work-related goals.

Compassion Fatigue, Burnout, and Compassion Satisfaction among Veterinary Technicians and Assistants

Both veterinary technicians and assistants are exposed to clients and patients. For the veterinarian, these exposures are positive and negative. The range and types of exposure depend on the job duties and how the positions function within the work setting.

Veterinary technicians' CF scores are slightly higher than those of veterinarians, and their reported stressors are different. Given role differences, these findings are to be expected (see Table 6.6).

Table 6.6—Compassion Fatigue of Veterinary Technicians and Assistants

Score	Risk Level	Percent Self-Reporting
41 or above	Extremely high risk	28.9
36–40	High risk	13.3
31–35	Moderate risk	10.0
27–30	Low risk	5.6
26 or below	Extremely low risk	42.2

Mail survey of 200 veterinarians' practices.
Source: HSUS 2003–2004.

The satisfaction from helping animals, teamwork, and "thankful clients" is the same for both veterinary technicians and veterinarians.

In this population 52.2 percent of those surveyed are between moderate and extremely high risk for CF. This CF level is extremely close to that of veterinarians, 54.3 percent. Once again, we see that CF is widespread. To learn more about stress, the survey asked veterinary technicians and assistants to list their top three sources of stress. The results of this survey are presented in Table 6.7.

Once again, difficult clients are the top stressor in the practice workplace. Veterinary technicians and veterinarians also share "not enough time" to devote to the animal. It is interesting to observe that problems with "co-workers" is a second-place stressor. In all likelihood, when there is greater co-worker interaction, more frequent conflict results.

Table 6.7—External Stressors of Veterinary Technicians and Assistants

Source of Stress	Percent Reporting
Difficult or noncompliant clients	42.6
Problems with co-workers	39.3
Not enough time	27.9
Performing euthanasia	24.6
Very ill or high-risk patients	19.7
Disputes with supervisor	18.0
Lack of sufficient trained staff	16.4
Losing a patient	11.5
Fractious or dangerous animals	9.8
Other (e.g., noise, computer problems)	9.8

Mail survey of 200 veterinarians' practices . (Multiple answers could be chosen.)
Source: HSUS 2003–2004.

Table 6.8—Sources of Compassion Satisfaction for Veterinary Technicians and Assistants

Source of Satisfaction	Percent Reporting
Helping/healing animals	82.0
Working as a team	48.9
Thankful clients	45.9
Using skills/learning new ones	41.0
Daily contact with animals	24.6
Educating clients	23.0

Mail survey of 200 veterinarians' practices. (Multiple answers could be chosen.)
Source: HSUS 2003–2004.

Veterinary technicians' and assistants' compassion satisfaction is directly related to animal care. The ability to help the patient is most important to these workers. The survey asked them to list their top three job satisfaction items. The compassion satisfaction of veterinary technicians and assistants is presented in Table 6.8.

The satisfaction from helping animals, teamwork, and "thankful clients" is the same for both veterinary technicians and veterinarians. It is also not surprising that new skill development is very important among technicians, as is time spent educating clients.

In examining burnout in technicians and assistants, the picture is extremely positive, and the low score here completes the bookend picture, which is very similar to the veterinarians'. Burnout in this population is presented in Table 6.9.

Table 6.9—Burnout in Veterinary Technicians and Assistants

Score	Risk Level	Percent Self-Reporting
76–85	Extremely high risk	1.1
51–75	High risk	6.7
37–50	Moderate risk	24.4
36 or below	Extremely low risk	67.8

Mail survey of 200 veterinarians' practices.
Source: HSUS 2003–2004.

Burnout has been defined as the general feeling of exhaustion that develops when a person simultaneously experiences too much pressure and has too few sources of satisfaction. The above data confirm that burnout is a moderate workplace issue for these positions. When employees say, "I am burned out," they are really recognizing, feeling, and expressing compassion fatigue. Compassion fatigue is very different from burnout. The problem is that technicians do not know about compassion fatigue. This lack of insight is not their fault; it is a result of the general widespread use of the term, burnout.

Compassion Fatigue, Burnout, and Compassion Satisfaction Within Veterinary Front Office Staff and Practice Management

Front office and practice management are exposed to both clients and patients. As with other positions within the practice setting, these exposures include positive *and* negative client interactions. The range and types of client exposure depend on job duties and how the positions function within the work setting. In many cases, front office staff members are the first point of contact with the client. This contact may take place in a reception area where there are many clients and patients. The presence of multiple clients, patients, incoming phone calls, and noise makes this work setting unique in the practice setting. Front office staff may also have less formal training in veterinary medicine.

Front office staff members report the lowest CF score within the practice setting, probably because they are much less often exposed to direct touching and treatment. CF scores for front office staff are reported in Table 6.10.

To learn more about stress, the survey asked front office staff members and practice management to list their top three sources of stress.

Increased client exposure replaces exposure to animals for individuals in these positions. Regarding disputes over fees, in all

---

Table 6.10—Compassion Fatigue of Front Office and Practice Management

Score	Risk Level	Percent Self-Reporting
41 or above	Extremely high risk	20.8
36–40	High risk	12.5
31–35	Moderate risk	8.3
27–30	Low risk	8.3
26 or below	Extremely low risk	50.0

Mail survey of 200 veterinarians' practices.
Source: HSUS 2003–2004.

Table 6.11—Stressors on Front Office and Practice Management

Stressor	Percent Reporting
Difficult or noncompliant clients	53.1
Time demands	46.9
Disputes over fees/billing	31.3
Office stressors (e.g., noise, computer problems)	25.0
Understaffed/staff training	15.6
Discussing euthanasia with clients	15.6
Abusive/neglectful clients	15.6
Problems with supervisors	15.6

Mail survey of 200 veterinarians' practices. (Multiple answers could be chosen.)
Source: HSUS 2003–2004.

likelihood the medical practitioner fills out the treatment and billing form and instructs the client "to take it to the front desk." It is here where the least-prepared person must discuss the fee. This exchange exacerbates any problems in relationships with difficult clients.

Table 6.12—Job Satisfiers for Front Office and Practice Management

Source of Satisfaction	Percent Reporting
Thankful clients	62.5
Daily contact with animals	59.4
Helping/healing animals	56.3
Working as a team	37.5
Using skills/learning new ones	25.0
Educating clients	25.0

Mail survey of 200 veterinarians' practices. (Multiple answers could be chosen.)
Source: HSUS 2003–2004.

Table 6.13—Burnout in Front Office and Practice Management

Score	Risk Level	Percent Self-Reporting
76–85	Extremely high risk	0.0
51–75	High risk	6.3
37–50	Moderate risk	16.7
36 or below	Extremely low risk	77.0

Mail survey of 200 veterinarians' practices.
Source: HSUS 2003–2004.

Job Satisfiers for Front Office and Practice Management

To learn more about job satisfaction, the survey asked front office staff members and practice management their top three on-the-job satisfiers.

Once again, the themes of thankful clients, helping animals, and teamwork emerge to add to compassion satisfaction within the practice setting. The paradox for front office employees is that interaction with the client is about equally positive and negative.

Given that these positions have the least medical training and are perhaps at the lowest entry level, it is expected that these areas would have the lowest BO rate within the practice setting. BO exposure scores are reported in Table 6.13.

While not questioning the dedication of these workers, it is clear that their emotional investment is not so great as that of the medical staff.

Conclusion

This chapter opened with four "fast facts," which became the recurring themes in the study of compassion fatigue, compassion satisfaction, and burnout in the practice of veterinary medicine. On the positive side, the love of and caring for animals was seen throughout the practice setting as the greatest source of CS. The relationship with "thankful clients" also recurred as a source of CS, as did the positive power of teamwork within the practice environment. On the negative side, the number-one source of CF was clearly difficult clients. Time demands were also a major contributor to CF within the practice setting.

To reduce CF in the practice setting, there must be a coherent plan to deal proactively with difficult clients.

The Connection

Debbie had an affection for animals all of her life. She was always bringing home stray cats, injured birds, snakes, toads, etc. So, it was no surprise when she decided to go to school to become a veterinary technician. She wanted to help save lives and heal the sick and injured animals of the world.

After working in an animal emergency room, doing exactly what she wanted to do, Debbie became discouraged by the nighttime and weekend hours and the low pay. She was a twenty-two-year-old with no social life and few friends because of her schedule. Debbie left the animal emergency room and went to work for her local animal control.

There she was, once again, picking up stray, sick and injured animals, only this time she was taking them to the animal shelter. But since this was a municipal shelter, there would be no medicine, no bandages, no veterinary care to heal the sick or wounded. Debbie would do her best with home remedies and makeshift medical supplies. She spent time comforting the fearful.

If they were lucky, the sheltered animals were claimed by their owner or perhaps adopted. Those less fortunate or those that were infirm had to be euthanized, which was a task that Debbie also had to perform. She had to kill the animals she tried to heal.

> *Although she did save lives, rescuing dogs from hot cars, cats from neglectful situations, nursing orphaned babies, all Debbie could focus on were the lives she couldn't save. And with each life she took, she became more and more disheartened. (Humane Society University 2001, 5)*

Should the above scenario be classified as "professional burnout" or as compassion fatigue? This is an example of someone working in her chosen profession and having to cope with physical or emotional pain. Is this example any different from animal caregivers' in her personal and emotional experiences? They all see pain, suffering, and death, and they all feel the effects of what they see.

The animal caregiver continues to provide care, despite a higher-than-expected rate of compassion fatigue. Despite the emotional and physical pressures, the animal caregiver returns to work day after day. At some point, the physical surroundings and the multiple emotional relationships, both human and non-human, take a cumulative toll.

Why do the animal caregivers return to work? They love what they do; however, at the same time, it hurts them. Why would one continue to work in a profession or do something that causes pain? This is a complex question whose answer lies in the relationship between the caregiver and the recipients of their care.

In general, animal caregivers provide care to two classes of animals—those with human companions and those without.

As previously discussed, the level of compassion fatigue for those individuals working in shelters and animal-control capacities is higher than for those working in the veterinary field. No existing research explains this discrepancy. As with any original inquiry, the initial explanation is usually "self-case reporting" or anecdotal (Barker 1999). The answer may be found in the different work setting, the absence or the presence of a human companion, or the health and prognosis of the animal. Despite the different settings, their common trait is the relationship between the caregiver and the animals. According to Gilman and Shepherd (1992), workers in the animal-shelter and animal-control fields are likely to develop anthropomorphism or misanthropy.

Anthropomorphism is the assignment of human characteristics to non-humans. Within this dynamic, the animal caregiver envisions the animal as a human. A classic example is when holding a puppy, a person says, "He is my baby." Gilman and Shepherd (1992) conclude that, once the animal has taken on human characteristics, the pressure to do what is in the best interest of the animal versus what the caregiver wants to do intensifies. This is a natural internal conflict within the caregiver. At the heart of the conflicts lies the question, "Do I do what I want to do, or do I do what is in the best interest of the animal?" This conflict can cause tremendous stress because one does not want to hurt his or her "baby." Within the shelter setting, caregivers work with the same animals on a continuous basis for an extended period of time. Therefore, the one-on-one relationship makes anthropomorphism all the more likely. In the veterinary setting, relationships and contacts change daily. While the veterinary worker might say, "How are you today, big boy?" the relationship is more transactional rather than long-term.

> Why do the animal caregivers return to work? They love what they do; however, at the same time, it hurts them.

In the HSUS survey (2003–2004), shelter workers were repeatedly asked three questions, the first of which was, "How many of you talk to animals?" The answer was 100 percent affirmative. The response was generally lighthearted and good natured. The typical conversation was, "You are a good boy," or "Would you like to go for a walk?" Talking to animals is seen as natural and something we all do.

The second question was, "How many have animals talk to you?" 100 percent of those questioned reported that animals talk to them. Once more, these responses were lighthearted and good natured. The caregivers are happy to admit that there is a two-way conversation going on and that is perfectly natural. Within the shelter setting where animals may be housed for weeks—or even months—as a result of long-term exposure and conversations, a relationship is established. On the other hand, the veterinary worker's conversation is brief and lasts no longer than the length of the appointment.

The last question posed to this population was, "How many of you lie to the animals, telling them everything is going to be okay, when you know that is not the case?" Generally, the mood quickly moves from lighthearted to somber, everyone's hand is raised. When asked why they lie to these loved ones, the responses are, "I do not want them to worry," or "I care for them too much," or "They do not need to know the truth," or "I do not want them to suffer anymore."

Figure 7.1—The Contagious Nature of Compassion Fatigue

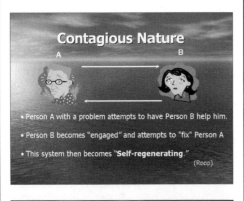

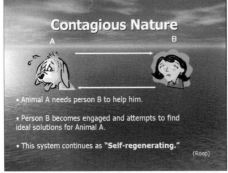

Source: Adapted from Gentry and Zaparanek 2003.

These responses clearly separate the shelter and animal-control professional from the veterinary worker.

Another distinction between the shelter and animal-care professional and the caregiver within the veterinary practice is the relationship with human caregivers. One dynamic is misanthropy—a dislike or mistrust of humans. According to Gilman and Shepard (1992, 8), "An excessive 'hating people' or 'loving animals more than people' attitude can do nothing but harm to animal-care and -control workers." They add, "Certainly everyone in the animal-care and -control field knows that people are to blame, and it is difficult to be nice to those at the heart of the problem." This emotion develops as the caregiver continuously deals with animal abuse and neglect.

While neglect and abuse occur in the practice setting, misanthropy is less likely to occur in veterinary caregivers, since the frequency of neglect and abuse is lower than in shelters and animal control.

Misanthropy and anthropomorphism add stress to the workplace and can spread to other staff members. These organization-wide feelings can lead to the animal caregiver developing compassion fatigue.

Robbins (2005) has demonstrated the effects of stress both on the individual and on overall organization performance. As stress increases, individual performance increases. There is an optimal point in the relationship at which stress is high and performance is increased. After that point, however, performance decreases rapidly.

Since an organization is made up of individuals, each at a different stress point, the organization can never reach its optimal potential due to various individual stress-related performance declines.

In the caregiving organization, this situation is compounded not only by stress, but also by the onset of compassion fatigue, which is passed from caregiver to caregiver. As the caregiver reaches out to a co-worker or to an animal to relieve painful emotions, the co-worker absorbs some of that person's pain. This is the contagious nature of compassion fatigue: people pass it to their co-workers in an attempt to seek relief. In seeking relief, everyone in the workplace becomes a potential victim (Roop and Vitelli 2003).

The central point in compassion fatigue and in all animal caregivers is the emotional bond between the caregiver and the animal. How these emotions help shape and establish the relationship determines the presence of compassion fatigue. All animal caregivers must realize they have chosen an "at-risk" profession. When we see animals with a good prognosis, we are happy. When we see animals who have been abused and neglected, we feel angry and disgusted. The range of these emotions is called the emotion continuum (Robbins 2005).

In explaining emotions, Robbins states:

> One way to classify them is by whether they are positive or negative. Positive emotions express a favorable feeling. Negative emotions express the opposite. Emotions can't be neutral. Importantly, negative emotions seem to have a greater effect on people. (2005, 115)

Animal caregivers in the shelter and animal-control professions seem to be exposed to more negative situations than are their counterparts in the veterinary profession. "People reflect on and think about events inducing strong negative emotions five times as long as they do about events inducing strong positive ones" (Robbins 2005, 115).

The widespread nature of compassion fatigue can be directly traced to the negative situations and negative emotions that all animal caregivers encounter.

PART III
REVITALIZATION AND RESILIENCE

Now What?

CHAPTER

The demand to be compassionate hour after hour, in all kinds of happy and sad situations, is a requirement for animal-care workers, but it can lead to stress. Stress is partly psychological and physiological. Psychological stress is a demand to manage a stressor, such as a looming board meeting, an upcoming cruelty case—nearly anything that demands our attention and action. Some stressors are very provocative but cause only short-term distress. Disasters, for example, require animal-care workers to search, rescue, and care for homeless animals. Yet most of these workers, despite the rigors of their actions in the field, will be fine. (They would be better, of course, if given sufficient TLC while in the field and upon their return.)

Other traumatic events can be very demanding but still leave people with positive feelings associated with the satisfaction of a job well done. The same stressor can cause joy, pride, and a connection with fellow survivors and still be a potentially traumatizing event. Crisis is neither positive nor negative with respect to immediate and long-term psychosocial consequences. A crisis can be a "dangerous opportunity," as noted by the Chinese, open to positive reactions, negative reactions, or (as is most often the case) a mixture of both.

Psychological stress is the need to manage the memory of a traumatizing stressor, no matter how recent the event may be. Traumatic stress is the need to manage a crisis or the memory of a traumatic crisis. Animal caregivers experience at least five crises a week—sometimes all in a single day. Some of those crises may be traumatic because of the nature of the situation—how dangerous and harmful it could have been—while other events are far from traumatic. Animal caregivers can experience traumatic stress when confronting memories of the event.

Revitalization and resilience are possible when facing compassion fatigue and other work-related distress. If you are an animal-care worker, the work you love can be toxic and requires you to help yourself and other animal caregivers by being proactive.

> The work you love can be toxic and requires you to help yourself and other animal caregivers by being proactive.

You are heroes to the rest of us. You take care of our "children" year in and year out, although you are often invisible to the public. Only in times of disaster do the drama and trauma of rescuing and protecting pets show up all too visibly in news reports. The lost animals roaming the streets of New Orleans after Hurricane Katrina in 2005 symbolized the animals you assist every day in every city and town in America.

You stand in the way of more suffering by doing your best every day. This work is emotionally difficult at times. Some animal-care workers neglect themselves because their needs come after those of the animals for whom they feel responsible.

You now know the classic signs of compassion fatigue: reduced sleep, irritability, crying spells, physical fatigue. Your co-workers and family members confirm what you already know: your job takes a toll, and you require special treatment that can neutralize the toxins.

There are short- and long-term routes to revitalizing yourself and thriving in your job. Answering the following questions is the first step.

- What is your level of compassion satisfaction for life generally? For your work as an animal-care professional?
- What are your plans for increasing your work satisfaction?
- How do you calm yourself at work? How do you purge distress, sadness, and difficult thoughts while on the job so you can carry on your important work?
- When you are away from work physically, are you away psychologically? How do you find joy in life? Do you have activities that counteract, and enable you to recover from, the stress at work?

■ How committed are you to self-care? How will you know when
your program of self-care is not working? What guidelines do
you follow to ensure your own self-care as an animal-care
professional?

Now let's turn our attention to each set of questions. As you will
see, the answers must come from you. However, we can get you
started thinking about what is in your own best interests.

The Work of Animal Care and Compassion Satisfaction

What is your level of compassion satisfaction for life
generally, and for your work as an animal-care
professional?

There are good days and bad days. On the bad days you need to be
able to turn to someone or something—either internally or externally—
that increases your level of satisfaction with this work, to remind you
that you are good at what you do and what you do is very important
to many people and animals. What are your plans for increasing your
work satisfaction? For example, you could make a sign you see every
day that reads: "Animals smile a lot here" or "I am good at what I do
and it shows." Find something that reminds you why you are doing
this work, that the successes and joys far outnumber the failures or
setbacks.

Stress Management at Work

How do you calm yourself at work? Some people take a smoke
break. Some pray. Some go outside and scream. Others
meditate, practice visualization, or use some other method
that reduces their stress and makes it more manageable. However, if
you do not have a stress management method that works well, here
are a few to try.

Breathing Exercises

More people use some version of this approach than any other,
because most people have discovered the benefits of breathing deeply.
They notice that when they experience periods of stress, their
breathing becomes shallow, and deeper breathing follows enjoyable

moments such as laughter. One of the simpler and more useful methods is offered by Ross (1988) in *The Wellness Workbook*. Here are her simple instructions:

- Sit down or lie down.
- Inhale slowly and say to yourself, *"I am..."*
- Exhale slowly and say to yourself, *"relaxed."*

Gradually consider the advantage of allowing yourself to breathe smoothly and naturally. Consider that when you breathe this way and stop thinking about your stressors, your breathing becomes even deeper. Keep in mind that the problem will not go away as you focus on your breathing. However, this exercise will enable you to take a break from the problem, calm yourself, and come back to the problem with greater energy and mental clarity. The more effective you are in learning how to breathe and manage stress better, the more effective you will be in solving the problems. So give yourself a break from your problems and stress just long enough to practice this exercise several times.

- Exhale deeply, contracting your belly.
- Inhale slowly as you expand your abdomen.
- Continue inhaling as you expand your chest.
- Continue inhaling as you raise your shoulders up toward your ears.
- Hold for a few comfortable seconds.
- Exhale in reverse pattern, slowly. Release your shoulders, relax your chest, contract your belly.
- Repeat.

Try to do this exercise before or after a meal and at bedtime.

Safe and Joyful Place (SJP) Visualization

This approach induces relaxation by using guided imagery. This can be either self-guided or guided by someone else (a person or a recording). The procedures vary, but here is a typical set of instructions.

The purpose of safe place visualization is to induce relaxation quickly by following the steps below. The more you practice, the quicker and more deeply relaxation takes effect.

- First, think of all the things you love, that comfort you, that trigger feelings of comfort, satisfaction, and lack of stress. Let any image like that come forward. Now think about it; doesn't

thinking about these places frequently bring a smile to your face?
- Next, think of a specific or imagined place that is safe, joyful, and serene. This will be your "Safe and Joyful Place" (SJP).
- Now bring up that SJP place and do the following:
  - Imagine smells, sounds, sensations—everything about the place—using all of your senses.
  - Focus on what it looks like when you look straight above where you are in your SJP.
  - Then focus on things to the right and then to the left.
  - Then allow yourself to go to a place in your mind that brings you the greatest peace, restfulness, and joy possible.
  - While you are at your SJP and mindful of these good thoughts, you are neutralizing the toxins of your work. Imagine that these toxic by-products of caregiving are a kettle on a stove. Give it a color, such as dark green, and imagine that you are dropping into the kettle drops of memories and sensations of joy and satisfaction derived from many sources. Each drop dilutes and eventually neutralizes the toxic by-products of caring for the suffering.
  - Now focus (as long as you need to) on the joy, restfulness, zest, and contentment of loving life in the fullest associated within that special place, while checking from time to time the color of the toxic substance. Stop when the substance is almost clear.
  - Now, after taking as much time as you need, gradually return to reality and the tasks of the day. Feel free to linger, thinking about ways to relax more in the face of work-related stress and that you deserve to rid yourself of the toxic effects of suffering patients.

Self-Hypnosis

This approach evokes a relaxed consciousness and focus that enables some to overcome stress linked to various stimuli (stressors). It is best used with animal caregivers who can focus on (1) their own situation and not depend on others to fix it; (2) recent crisis events rather than those that happened in the distant past; (3) issues associated with their feelings and anxiety, rather than on their performance; and (4) issues needing new cognitions—thoughts, attitudes, or images—not problems requiring insight or new knowledge. These last can be addressed by therapy and education, respectively.

Do not use self-hypnosis with (1) issues best helped by a professional mental health specialist, such as serious, long-term mental illness; (2) interpersonal issues (better handled through couple or group hypnosis); or (3) poorly motivated people who are unwilling to put in the time every day to be successful in stress reduction. Following is a form of self-hypnosis adapted from Henderson (2003).

Self-Talk, Self-Advice

First, decide what advice you wish to give to yourself and put it in the form of a positive statement. For example, you could say: "Slow down and enjoy life," or "Be happy, don't worry," or "Turn a negative into a positive." Be creative but make it advice you really want to take and let it be a guide for you. Write your suggestion(s) below (see item 18).

Second, make a tape recording of yourself reading the following statements. Once you have made the recording, play it at least once a day at a time when you can relax and concentrate undisturbed for thirty minutes. Don't worry if you fall asleep listening.

Third, read the following statements below:

1. My name is _____. I care about myself deeply and completely and know that when I am at my best, I am more effective as a caregiver. I choose to reserve the following thirty minutes to myself.

2. I am starting my self-talk session now. It will continue until I hear myself say, "attention." In the meantime I will get more and more relaxed and focus more and more on my voice. I will give myself advice. This advice will be effective only if I want it to be effective.

3. I will now close my eyes and focus my attention on lying down on a comfortable bed in a very safe and comforting place that I know about. This special place allows me complete privacy, safety, and comfort.

4. In my safe place, lying on my safe and comfortable bed, I can feel a warm, magic quilt covering my feet. This quilt is covered with material representing the best scenes from my life in which I felt love, caring, and joy. As a result of being covered, my feet are becoming more and more relaxed.

5. When I am ready, my feet will become more and more relaxed as I pull the quilt up to cover my lower legs. When I do so,

my lower legs start to become more and more relaxed. My feet are becoming even more deeply relaxed, followed closely by my lower legs. All of the muscles in my feet and lower legs are becoming limp and relaxed.

6. When I am ready, I will pull the magic quilt over my knees. Now they begin to feel relaxed and soon feel as relaxed as my lower legs and feet. Every muscle and tendon in my knees and below them is becoming more and more relaxed. All tension is flowing out of this area, leaving all the muscles limp and loose.

7. Sometimes I may hear noises or have thoughts that attract my attention. I will just gently let them go away because this time is reserved for just me. I am thinking only of relaxing and letting go of all tension. All of my muscles are becoming more and more relaxed, and I am feeling pleasantly drowsy. I will not go to sleep. I will remain alert but feeling more and more relaxed. I am sinking further and further into myself with no cares or worries.

> Decide what advice you wish to give to yourself and put it in the form of a positive statement.

8. When I am ready, I will pull the magic quilt over my upper legs. Now they begin to feel relaxed and soon feel as relaxed as the area below them. Every muscle and tendon in my upper legs and below them is becoming more and more relaxed. All tension is flowing out of this area, leaving all the muscles limp and loose.

9. When I am ready, I will pull the magic quilt up over my stomach and just below my chest. Now my stomach begins to feel relaxed and soon feels as relaxed as the areas below. Every muscle and tendon in the areas below my chest is becoming more and more relaxed. All tension is flowing out of this area, leaving all the muscles limp and loose.

10. When I am ready, I will pull the magic quilt up over my arms and chest, just below my neck. Now my arms and chest begin to feel relaxed and soon feel as relaxed as the areas below them. Every muscle and tendon in the areas below my neck is becoming more and more relaxed. All tension is flowing out of this area, leaving all the muscles limp and loose.

11. The relaxation is like warmth, spreading to every place

covered by my magic quilt. The muscles in the covered area are becoming limper. I could move if I really had to, but I am becoming so comfortably limp and relaxed that I don't want to move. I am still and relaxed, drifting deeper and deeper into a pleasant state of dreamy relaxation.

12. When I am ready, I will pull the magic quilt up over my neck, leaving just my head exposed. Now my neck begins to feel relaxed and soon feels as relaxed as the areas below it. Every muscle and tendon in this area covered by my quilt is becoming more and more relaxed. All tension is flowing out of this area, leaving all the muscles limp and loose.

13. Even though my magic quilt remains below my head, now the relaxation is spreading into my mouth and jaw muscles. My tongue is limp, resting in my mouth. I may briefly have more saliva in my mouth, but that will go away shortly. Now my cheeks and eyes are relaxing. I could open my eyes if I wanted to, but unless I need to, it would be too much work. It would take too much effort to open my eyes. I am drifting pleasantly downward, becoming more and more relaxed.

14. The muscles in my forehead are becoming more and more relaxed. I can imagine them, like loosening rubber bands across my forehead, becoming limp and floppy. I am feeling deeper and deeper relaxation. From the tips of my toes to the top of my head, I am becoming more and more relaxed, drifting downward, deeper and deeper.

15. When I am ready, I am going to count down from twenty-five. As I count down, I will continue to become more and more relaxed and pleasantly deeper and deeper into relaxation. I will get drowsy and deeply relaxed, but I will not actually go to sleep. I will simply drift deeper and deeper into my self-hypnotic state of deeply relaxed awareness.

16. By the time I reach zero, I will be in a very pleasant, sleeplike state. I will still be able to direct my thoughts. I could rouse myself immediately if I needed to, but if not, I will give myself a break. I will continue to drift deeper and deeper into relaxation.

17. When I am ready, I will attend to the counting:...twenty-five...twenty-four...twenty-three...twenty-two...drifting deeper and deeper with each number...twenty-one...twenty...feeling drowsier and drowsier, yet still awake...nineteen...eighteen...

seventeen...floating gently downward with each count...
sixteen...fifteen...fourteen...drifting, drowsy...thirteen...twelve..
eleven...ten...more than halfway down, drifting deeper and
deeper with each number...nine...eight...seven...six...five...
feeling so relaxed...four...becoming more and more relaxed
and drowsy...three...two...one...zero. Breathing pleasantly,
slowly, drifting deeper and deeper with each breath.

18. As I continue to be deeply relaxed and become even more
relaxed, I am thinking about my advice: [At this point insert
your advice to yourself]:

_____

_____

_____

_____

19. All of the advice I give myself, I do so out of love and self-
caring. I know that this is good advice and that my life and
my work will be better as a result of following it.

20. Each time I practice this self-talk exercise, I will become better
and better at it. I will be able to relax deeper and deeper in less
time with each practice.

21. Now, as I count to three, I am going to slowly, gradually,
pleasantly wake up and come to attention. I will return to my
normal, waking state, except that I'll be far more alert and
relaxed than before and fully aware of my self-advice. Now,
starting up...one...becoming more alert...two...getting ready to
wake up...three, wake up.

22. I congratulate myself for taking this time for my self-care and
will be thinking often of my own advice throughout the day
and even when I sleep.

Gestalt Chair Technique

This approach enables you to become aware of and deal with any "unfinished business" of expressing anger, forgiveness, and other issues that involuntarily occupy your mind.

Table 8.1—Six-Step Gestalt Chair Technique

Step	Purpose	Activities
1	**Preparation**	■ Arrange two chairs facing each other. ■ Clarify the goals and offending person.
2	**Relaxation**	■ Use your most effective stress-reduction method. ■ Prepare yourself to be fully present and focused on the tasks to follow.
3	**Imagine the Offender**	■ Focus all your attention on the other chair and imagine the offender sitting there and what the person would look like, how he or she would be sitting there.
4	**Statements to the Offender**	■ Start by saying something positive (e.g., I know your criticisms come from your heart and you never intend to hurt my feelings). ■ State your intention (e.g., I am talking with you today to resolve unfinished business between us and not to intentionally hurt you), then what you hope to get from these exchanges (e.g., peace of mind, a sense of satisfaction). ■ Tell the offender what you are thinking and feeling in detail, starting with what happened and its effects. ■ Cover as many issues and points as are relevant. ■ Remain seated and experience your feelings as much as possible—let them all come out, without holding back.

Step	Purpose	Activities
5	**Statements by the Offender**	■ Trade seats. ■ Immerse yourself in the point of view and personality of the offender—hopes, disappointments, fears, frustrations, hurts. ■ Allow the offender to respond to your statements. ■ Remain fully focused on the offender's perspective.
6	**Continue to Change Seats and Perspectives**	■ Allow any and all issues to come forward. ■ Allow each party to respond fully. ■ Continually absorb the full experience and sensations of the exchange. ■ Stay with your feelings and check with the other person regarding full understanding.
7	**Final Statement**	■ Allow each person to express what he or she has learned and how things will change (or not change) as a consequence of this exchange.

A useful variation is to videotape the exchange. Remain in one chair but change the camera (close up for own self, farther away for the offender) to differentiate roles. After videotaping, play the tape back and tape the response, etc.

Acupressure Stress Reduction (ASR) Technique

This approach induces relaxation by stimulating various pressure points on the upper torso that are associated with stress reactions.

Table 8.2—Twenty-One Step Acupressure Stress Reduction (ASR) Technique

Step	Purpose	Activities
1	**Review of Distressing Stressors**	■ Think of the cause of your anxiety (we all have it from time to time) and work up as much discomfort as you can. Do not spend more than a few moments on this phase.
2	**Body Scan**	■ Briefly think about your entire body, from top to bottom, and note any unaccounted-for sensations (e.g, ringing in ears, neck tension). ■ Make a mental note of these sensations and look for them again when you are fully relaxed.
3	**Assessment 1: Identifying Your Stress Level**	■ Focus on the stressor and your level of stress here and now. ■ Choose a number between one and ten that best represents the intensity of your discomfort, with ten being the highest level of distress possible at the moment and one being the lowest level, the most relaxed possible. Then circle the number below: 1.....2.....3.......4.....5......6.......7......8.....9.....10
4	**Tapping Area 1**	■ Using two fingers (of either hand), tap the side of the other hand (below the little finger) while saying: "I accept myself fully and completely even though I am stressed about _____ [insert stressor here]." Repeat this statement three times while continuing to tap.
5		■ Tap solidly five times under your eyes, using two fingertips of each hand. Think about the stressor while you continue to tap.
6		■ Tap just above the bridge of your nose, approximately where either eyebrow begins.
7		■ Use your thumbs to tap under your arms, approximately four inches below your armpits. ■ Use two fingers again to tap on your chest just below the collarbone, approximately one inch on either side from the center of your chest.

Step	Purpose	Activities
8	Assessment 2	■ Take a deep breath and measure your anxiety again: Choose a number between one and ten that best represents the intensity of your anxiety right now. Then circle the number below: 1......2......3.......4.......5......6........7......8......9......10 If your level is higher than two, continue to the next step.
9	Tapping Area 2	■ In this phase you tap only one spot (inside the "V"-shaped web created by the little finger and the one next to it) just below the knuckles from the fingers, while simultaneously doing the following:
10		■ Close eyes.
11		■ Open eyes.
12		■ Look down to the right.
13		■ Look down to the left.
14		■ Move your eyes in a circle.
15		■ Move your eyes in a circle in the other direction.
16		■ Hum any tune that makes you smile (e.g., "Happy Birthday").
17		■ Count to five.
18		■ Hum the tune again.
19		■ Count to five again.
20	Assessment 3	■ Take a deep breath and measure your anxiety again: Choose a number between one and ten that best represents the intensity of your anxiety right now. Then circle the number below: 1......2......3.......4.......5......6........7......8......9......10 If your level now is higher than two, continue to the next step.
21	Decision Point	■ If your distress level is two or higher, repeat steps 4–20 until it is one.

The ASR approach is variously known as "thought field therapy," "emotion-focused therapy," and the "tapping technique."

Meditation

The purpose of meditation is to help animal caregivers who require time to themselves to heal naturally. It is not significantly different from prayer, but it does not require any particular religiously sanctioned protocol. It provides a time of high concentration on any challenges while experiencing peacefulness and mindfulness.

Table 8.3—Seven-Step Meditation Procedure

Step	Name	Direction
1	**Assessment 1: Identify Your Stress Level**	■ Focus on the stressor and your level of stress here and now. ■ Choose a number between one and ten that best represents the intensity of your discomfort, with ten being the highest level of distress possible at the moment and one being the lowest level of distress, the most relaxed possible. Then circle the number below: 1......2......3.......4......5......6.......7......8......9......10
2	**Establish Posture**	■ Center yourself in a comfortable place and position on the floor.
3	**Establish Physical Focus**	■ Close your eyes or fix on a spot on floor.
4	**Allow Mind to Wander but Also Focus on the Directions**	■ Focus on each breath.
5		■ Count each breath in cycles of four (concentrate on counting accurately).
6		■ Allow the sounds of the outside world to enter your consciousness but simply pass from your attention.
7	**Ending**	■ When your distress level is below two.
8	**Assessment 2: Identify Your Stress level**	■ Focus on the stressor and your level of stress here and now. ■ Choose a number between one and ten that best represents the intensity of your discomfort, with ten being the highest level of distress possible at the moment and one being the lowest level of distress; the most relaxed possible. Then circle the number below: 1......2......3.......4......5......6.......7......8......9......10

Rewind Technique

This technique enables animal caregivers to deal with at least one disturbing memory that leaves them with lasting intrusive and distressing images, sounds, and smells that continue to haunt and harm them. This version of the rewind technique is drawn from the explanation offered by D. Muss (2002), an English physician who discovered its power when attempting to recovery psychologically from a skiing accident.

Table 8.4—Eight-Step Rewind Technique

Step	Name	Direction
1	**Assessment 1: Identify Your Stress Level**	■ Focus on the stressor and your level of stress here and now. ■ Choose a number between one and ten that best represents the intensity of your discomfort, with ten being the highest level of distress possible at the moment and one being the lowest level of distress,the most relaxed possible. Then circle the number below: 1......2.....3........4......5......6........7......8.....9......10
2	**Set-up**	■ The rewind technique consists of imagining watching a film of your traumatic event in the exact way that it haunts you, first forward and then backward. Think of the procedure as a new game. You have rented an entire movie theater, and you are sitting in the front row watching a movie about your life. The scene is frozen (freeze frame) and is you, minutes before the traumatic event happens.
3	**Floating Out**	■ Imagine that you are floating out of your body so that you are able to see yourself. Close your eyes and keep them closed after you read the instructions. Alternatively, someone you trust can guide you by reading these instructions to you.
4	**Setting**	■ Imagine that you do this in a large theater and you float back from the front row where you are sitting to the projection booth. ■ From there you can see the entire theater of empty seats, except that you can see the back of your head as you sit in the front row looking up at the screen.

table continued

Table 8.4—Eight-Step Rewind Technique (continued)

Step	Name	Direction
5	**Film about the Event**	■ From the projection booth, you are able to control a film of your distressing memory. This film will be exactly as it happened, as if someone videotaped the entire event and is playing it for you for the first time. But the film starts sometime before the traumatic aspects of the event took place, and the film ends sometime after the event, when you are relaxed and feel safe again.
6	**Play the Film at Regular Speed**	■ Imagine playing the film and seeing it from the projection booth. You will see and hear all of the details and may even recall the smells and other sensations from the event. Feel free to move away from the little window, shut your eyes, or whatever you need to do to feel safe and be reminded that you are not actually there but here.
7	**The Rewind**	■ Imagine playing the film backward, but this time you are experiencing what it was like then, except backward. Also, the movement backward is very fast, and it is hard to tell exactly what is happening, but you lived it and know the reality as you imagine yourself moving backward quickly as that slice of your life is rewinding.
8	**Play Film Fast Forward**	■ Imagine watching the film as in Step 6 above except in fast-forward speed.
		■ Repeat steps 5–8 until your distress level is two or less. However, make sure that you did not avoid the most distressing aspects in the film.
9	**Ending**	■ There is no need to continue to practice the technique, but do notice what happens over the following weeks. Use this technique for any other traumatic events in your life, following the same procedure.

Group Activities

Peer Support: This approach provides an opportunity for animal-care workers and their families to discuss their personal and professional problems with one of their own who has received special training and can help colleagues seek help from other sources. Peer support must be sanctioned and encouraged by management. Ideally, peer support should originate with the worker rather than with management, especially when it is a requirement for working or avoiding being fired.[6]

Half of the material on peer support training includes rather generic strategies for working one-on-one with peers. The other half is on the culture of the context (e.g., animal-rescue shelters, animal rescue, euthanasia, and other responsibilities that are highly stressful). Among the generic strategies are the approaches we discuss in this part of the book.

Defusing: This approach provides an opportunity for animal-care workers to talk with someone, such as a peer who is trained in defusing technique, about a critical issue or crisis. Most often defusing appears to be a brief conversation between someone in crisis or who wants to talk about a crisis and his or her peer.

Table 8.5—Six-Step Defusing Model for Support, Reassurance, and Provision of Information (adapted by Kathy Regan Figley)

Step	Purpose	Activities
1	**Make Contact**	■ Begin with a social greeting. ■ Avoid condescending or trivializing comments. ■ Do *not* ask for a detailed account immediately.
2	**Make Assessment**	■ Determine the willingness of the individual to discuss his or her experience. ■ If practical concerns take precedence, ask open-ended questions. ■ Follow the "flow" of the other person's thoughts. ■ Evaluate the responses to questions about how the individual first became aware of the incident.
3	**Gather Facts**	■ Helpful questions: 　• What did you do during the initial hours? When? 　• What do you remember about the scene (e.g., sights, sounds, smells)? 　• How is this incident affecting you? 　• Is it affecting others in your life (work, home, social)?
4	**Inquire about Thoughts**	■ Use the facts shared by the individual to generate questions about associated thoughts. ■ Examples: 　• What were your first thoughts when the immediate danger was over? 　• What thoughts keep coming back to you?

Step	Purpose	Activities
5	**Inquire about Feelings**	■ Use the description of the individual's thoughts to inquire about feelings. ■ Example: • What was the most difficult part about the incident for you? • Assure the person that emotional reactions are normal for the type of incident experienced. ■ Use the description of the individual's thoughts to inquire about feelings. ■ Example: • What was the most difficult part about the incident for you? • Assure the person that the emotional reactions are normal for the type of incident experienced.
6	**Support, Reassure, and Provide Information**	■ Active listening ■ Information ■ Ongoing practical assistance as appropriate ■ Reassure the person that his or her reactions to the incident are normal to help minimize self-criticism, shame, and guilt.

Debriefing: This approach provides an opportunity for animal-care workers to talk with someone individually, such as a peer trained in defusing technique, or in a group of peers (groups should be as homogeneous as possible and should exclude management) in a rather formal process that enables participants to talk about any aspect of the traumatic event and their reactions to it. The purpose of psychological debriefing or "first aid" is to place one's experiences in a broader context, to recognize opportunities to learn from the event, and to suffer as few negative consequences as possible.

This kind of opportunity, especially when arranged and paid for by management, is an extremely powerful and preventive measure (Boscarino, Figley, and Adams 2005). Regehr and Hill (2002) provide guidelines for leading a defusing or crisis intervention.

The aim of crisis debriefing is fourfold: (1) to help the participants understand the relationship between the event and their reactions; (2) to provide an opportunity for cathartic release of feelings, thoughts, and emotions, as needed; (3) to identify successful coping strategies; and (4) to promote use of various support systems. Thus, crisis debriefing is only one element of a comprehensive plan to promote wellness and resilience.

The structure varies, but each crisis debriefing is conducted as part of a pyschoeducational group meeting in which a structured procedure is followed to allow individuals to process the crisis event and its aftermath. Crisis debriefing is not counseling or therapy; rather, it is an organized, group education process that encourages self disclosure, but participation is voluntary. The leader should be a peer who was not directly subjected to the crisis. The generic procedure follows.

Table 8.6—Five-Stage Crisis Debriefing Model

Stage	Purpose	Activities
1	**Reviewing the Event**	■ Participants are asked to describe the sights, sounds, smells, and physical sensations they experienced at the time. Collectively, the group constructs a comprehensive, firsthand description of what happened and why.
2	**Reviewing Reactions**	■ Participants are asked to describe their reactions to the event, including their behavior, emotions—and those of other survivors—and the reactions of family, friends, and other supporters.
3	**Coping and Resilience**	■ Participants are asked to describe their strategies and efforts to cope with the above information and reactions of themselves and others. Here is where the leader can suggest additional ways to increase coping and resilience.
4	**Constructing Healing Theories**	■ Participants are asked to describe their reactions and coping in the context of the entire event and its aftermath, especially what they have learned and accomplished along the way. Emphasis is on growth and resilience.
5	**Reengagement**	■ Participants are asked to describe how they anticipate going back to work and getting on with their lives after this crisis, including how long they think it will take them to recover and how patient they will be with themselves and others.

Stress Management away from Work

When you are away from work physically, are you away psychologically? Use the above individual procedures for calming yourself. In addition to these specific stress management techniques, however, you should have in your life a variety of ways to have fun, or at least activities that take your attention away from work matters. Hobbies, gardening, long bike rides, runs, and walks are examples of such activities. Listening to music, reading, praying, and playing with children or pets are also examples of activities that activate joy, fun, and inspiration.

Your Personal Program of Self-Care

The Commitment to Self-Care

Just as a New Year's resolution is easy to make but harder to follow, so is self-care. It starts with a commitment—both a written and oral statement witnessed by at least one person in your personal life and one person in your professional life.

Here are some examples of commitments to self-care:

> "I promise to treat myself at least as well as I treat my patients—physically and emotionally—and that means following the Academy's Standards of Self-Care."

> "I can help my clients best by being my best. Being my best requires doing the best things for me. Among those are getting enough sleep, good nutrition, breaks, and stress management. I promise I will attend to self-care as much as to the care of others."

> "I, too, deserve the best treatment by others and by myself, and I promise to do it."

The Academy of Traumatology's Standards of Self-Care, found below, emerged from careful analysis of the research and professional practice literature.

> When you are away from work physically, are you away psychologically?

A Simple Checklist

Please complete this checklist now, then every three months, to see how your self-care program is progressing.

How often did you do the following things in the last full week you worked?

Table 8.7—Self-Care Activity

	Self-Care Activity	Often	Occa-sionally	Rarely	Don't Know
1	Did not respect my own dignity or self-worth				
2	Took responsibility for self-care				
3	Self-care yielded to duty to perform				
4	Thought about my right to wellness				
5	Thought about my own physical rest and nourishment				
6	Thought about my own emotional rest and nourishment				
7	Thought about moderating food, drink, cigarettes, and other substances for my own health				
8	Sought, found, and remembered appreciation from supervisors and clients				
9	Made it known that I wish to be recognized for my service				
10	Made or remembered my formal, tangible commitment to self-care				
11	Set or recalled self-care plan deadlines and goals				
12	Thought about strategies for letting go of work				
13	Made a formal, tangible commitment				
14	Set deadlines and goals				
15	Generated strategies that work and followed them				
16	Thought about strategies for gaining a sense of achievement				

	Self-Care Activity	Often	Occa-sionally	Rarely	Don't Know
17	Thought about acquiring adequate rest and relaxation				
18	Practiced effective, daily stress-reduction method(s)				
19	Practiced effective physical exercise to improve my health				
20	Noticed and worked on my body to improve my health				
21	Practiced effective sleep induction and maintenance for better health				
22	Practiced proper nutrition for better health				
23	Practiced effective behaviors and practices that sustain balance between work and play				
24	Practiced effective relaxation time and methods				
25	Had contact with nature or other calming stimuli				
26	Practiced effective methods of creative expression				
27	Practiced effective skills for assertiveness				
28	Practiced effective skills for stress reduction				
29	Practiced effective skills for interpersonal communication				
30	Practiced effective skills for cognitive restructuring				
31	Practiced effective skills for time management				
32	Practiced effective skills and competence in meditation or spiritual practice that is calming				
33	Practiced effective methods of self-assessment and self-awareness				
34	Found social supports				

	Self-Care Activity	Often	Occa-sionally	Rarely	Don't Know
35	Got help				
36	Practiced social activism				
37	Balanced work and home				
38	Practiced boundaries/limit setting regarding work and personal time				
39	Practiced setting or retaining professional boundaries				
40	Practiced setting or retaining personal boundaries				
41	Effectively addressed the pressures of multiple roles				
42	Practiced realism about how much I can do in one day				
43	Found support/help at work through peer support				
44	Found support/help at work through supervision/consultation/therapy				
45	Interacted with role models/mentors				
46	Sought and noted indications and causes of work satisfaction				
47	Thought about improvements in my self-care plan				

Your completed checklist should indicate attention to your own self-care. If it does, then you are moving toward wellness. If it does not, then you are not trying to assume responsibility for your own care. As noted throughout this book, only you know best regarding the state of your health—mentally and medically—and how best to move toward wellness.

Final Thoughts

You and your fellow animal caregivers are a critical part of society because your work is very important. Yet, at the same time, your work is also heartbreaking and stressful. We hope that we have helped you recognize that a compassionate caregiver requires compassion in return; that it takes extraordinary energy to be effective; and that the toxic by-products of your work can zap your energy. We hope that this book provides you with insights about the challenges of this work and how to regain your energy. Please write us and let us know what worked, what didn't work, and how we can better help you with your very important job of animal care.

Note

[6] A peer support program (PSP) requires that at least 10 percent of any staff be trained to have sufficient support when required. For workers working in the wake of a disaster and responsible for the highly stressful work of rescuing and caring for homeless animals, the ratio of workers to PSP members should be five to one.

Appendix A

Academy of Traumatology Green Cross Standards
of Self-Care Guidelines

Standards	Comment
I. Purpose of the Guidelines	As with the standards of practice in any field, the practitioner is required to abide by standards of self-care. These guidelines are used by all members of the Green Cross. The purpose of the Guidelines is twofold: First, *do no harm to yourself* in the line of duty when helping/treating others. Second, attend to your physical, social, emotional, and spiritual needs as a way of ensuring high-quality services for those who look to you for support as a human being.
II. Ethical Principles of Self-Care in Practice	These principles declare that it is unethical *not* to attend to your self care as a practitioner because sufficient self-care prevents us from harming those we serve.
1. Respect for the dignity and worth of self	A violation lowers your integrity and trust.
2. Responsibility of self-care	Ultimately it is your responsibility to take care of yourself, and no situation or person can justify neglecting it.
3. Self-care and duty to perform	There must be a recognition that the duty to perform as a helper cannot be fulfilled if there is not, at the same time, a duty to self-care.

Standards	Comment
III. Standards of Humane Practice of Self-Care	
1. Universal right to wellness	Every helper, regardless of his or her role or employer, has a right to wellness associated with self-care.
2. Physical rest and nourishment	Every helper deserves restful sleep and physical separation from work that sustains him or her in his or her work role.
3. Emotional rest and nourishment	Every helper deserves emotional and spiritual renewal, both in and outside the work context.
4. Sustenance modulation	Every helper must use self-restraint with regard to what and how much he or she consumes (e.g., food, drink, drugs, stimulation), since it can compromise his or her competence as a helper.
IV. Standards for Expecting Appreciation and Compensation	
1. Seek, find, and remember appreciation from supervisors and clients	These and other activities increase workers' satisfaction and sustain them emotionally and spiritually in their helping.
2. Make it known that you wish to be recognized for your service	Recognition also increases workers' satisfaction, which sustains them.
3. Select one or more advocates	They are colleagues who know you as a person and as a helper and are committed to monitoring your efforts at self-care.
V. Standards for Establishing and Maintaining Wellness Section A. Commitment to Self-Care	
1. Make a formal, tangible commitment	Written, public, specific, and measurable promise of self-care.
2. Set deadlines and goals	The self-care plan should set deadlines and goals connected to specific self-care activities.
3. Generate strategies that work and follow them	Such a plan must be attainable, followed with great commitment, and monitored by advocates of your self-care.

Standards	Comment
Section B: Strategies for Letting Go of Work	
1. Make a formal, tangible commitment. Set deadlines and goals	Written, public, specific, and measurable promise of letting go of work in off-hours and embracing rejuvenation activities that are fun, stimulating, inspiring, and generate joy of life. The letting-go-of-work plan should set deadlines and goals connected to specific activities of self-care.
2. Generate strategies that work and follow them	Such a plan must be attainable, followed with great commitment, and monitored by advocates of your self-care.
Section C. Strategies for Gaining a Sense of Self-Care Achievement	
1. Strategies for acquiring adequate rest and relaxation	The strategies are tailored to your own interests and abilities, which result in rest and relaxation most of the time.
2. Strategies for practicing effective daily stress reduction method(s)	The strategies are tailored to your own interest and abilities to effectively manage your stress during working hours and off-hours, recognizing that they will probably be different strategies from others'.
VI. Inventory of Self-Care Practice—Personal Section A: Physical	
1. Body work	Effectively monitoring all parts of your body for tension and using techniques that reduce or eliminate such tensions.
2. Effective sleep induction and maintenance	An array of healthy methods that induce sleep and a return to sleep under a wide variety of circumstances, including noise, smells, and light.
3. Effective methods for ensuring proper nutrition	Effectively monitoring all food and drink intake and lack of intake with the awareness of their implications for health and functioning.
Section B: Psychological	
1. Effective behaviors and practices to sustain balance between work and play	Only you know the meaning and presence of effective behaviors and practices. Those who begin to actively say "no" and note that it is part of a program of transformation toward a better life display such behaviors and practices.

Standards	Comment
2. Effective relaxation time and methods	No matter how you practice to attain relaxation, just attaining it means that your method works. However, it is important to always be searching for a way that is more efficient and nearly effortless.
3. Frequent contact with nature or other calming stimuli	Hanging around an environment such as being with nature, sitting in your favorite room, in a hot tub, or other such places that invoke the relaxation response.
4. Effective methods of creative expression	Creative expression through art, for example, enables those with compassion fatigue to express their innermost fears and strengths. Effective art therapy programs should be every place where the traumatized gather.
5. Effective skills for ongoing self-care	
a. Assertiveness	
b. Stress reduction	
c. Interpersonal communication	
d. Cognitive restructuring	
e. Time management	
6. Effective skill and competence in meditation or spiritual practice that is calming	
7. Effective methods of self-assessment and self-awareness	
Section C: Social/Interpersonal	
Social supports	At least five people, including at least two at work who will be highly supportive when called on
Getting help	Knowing when and how to secure help—informal and professional—that will be delivered quickly and effectively
Social activism	Being involved in addressing or preventing social injustice that results in a better world and a sense of satisfaction in trying to make it so

Standards	Comment
VII. Inventory of Self-Care Practice—Professional	
1. Balance between work and home	Devoting sufficient time and attention to both without compromising either
2. Boundaries/limit setting	Making a commitment and sticking to it
3. Time boundaries/overworking	
4. Therapeutic/professional boundaries	
5. Personal boundaries	
6. Dealing with multiple roles (both social and professional)	
7. Realism in differentiating between things one can change and accepting those one can't change	
8. Getting support/help at work	
9. Peer support	
10. Supervision/consultation/therapy	
11. Role models/mentors	
12. Generating work satisfaction	By noticing and remembering the joys and achievements of the work
VIII. Prevention Plan Development	
Step One: Review current self-care and prevention functioning	Be as honest as you can. Think about the tests you completed and the lapses in self-care you tend to repeat frequently. For example, you may take work home with you and spend time working when you should be resting. You might not do what it takes to get sufficient sleep or may skip lunch or breaks.
Step Two: Select one goal from each category	The first goals should be more easily attainable than most of the others and would produce considerable satisfaction if achieved.
Step Three: Analyze the resources for and resistances to achieving goal	Sometimes we find that some of our goals are impossible to achieve, but we do not know it until we try. If so, the goal needs to be eliminated or changed to one that is achievable. Most often, however, we run into barriers that prevent us from reaching our goals. These barriers might be quite predictable or unpredictable.

Standards	Comment
Step Four: Discuss goal and implementation plan with support person	Your supporter can help you recognize whether the goal you selected is reasonable and be more prepared to overcome the barriers to attaining it.
Step Five: Activate plan	Take your time and implement your plans gradually. You have lived with poor self-care, and changing this pattern takes time.
Step Six: Evaluate plan weekly, monthly, yearly with support person	Assume that your plan will require changes; most plans do. Use the time and information acquired from implementing your plan to regularly evaluate and consider changes to the plan. It is likely that the plan will need many changes in the beginning months, but, with improvements, fewer changes will be needed.
Step Seven: Notice and appreciate the changes	Sometimes we do not savor our victories and achievements, and, as a result, we do not get the full benefit of our success. This can make a big difference when we are changing patterns of behavior that have been habits for many years. Ask your support person to help you figure out a way to celebrate reaching your goal and the changes that come with an effective self-care plan.

Appendix B
Compassion Satisfaction and Fatigue (CSF) Test

Helping others puts you in direct contact with other people's lives. As you probably have experienced, your compassion for those you help has both positive and negative aspects. This self-test helps you estimate your compassion status: How much at risk you are of burnout and compassion fatigue and also the degree of satisfaction with your helping others. Consider each of the following characteristics about you and your current situation. Write in the number that honestly reflects how frequently you experienced these characteristics in the last week. Then follow the scoring directions at the end of the self-test.

0=Never   1=Rarely   2=A Few Times   3=Somewhat Often   4=Often   5=Very Often

Items About You
_____ 1. I am happy.
_____ 2. I find my life satisfying.
_____ 3. I have beliefs that sustain me.
_____ 4. I feel estranged from others.
_____ 5. I find that I learn new things from those I care for.
_____ 6. I force myself to avoid certain thoughts or feelings that remind me of a frightening experience.
_____ 7. I find myself avoiding certain activities or situations because they remind me of a frightening experience.
_____ 8. I have gaps in my memory about frightening events.
_____ 9. I feel connected to others.
_____ 10. I feel calm.

_____11. I believe that I have a good balance between my work and my free time.

_____12. I have difficulty falling or staying asleep.

_____13. I have outbursts of anger or irritability with little provocation.

_____14. I am the person I always wanted to be.

_____15. I startle easily.

_____16. While working with a victim, I thought about violence against the perpetrator.

_____17. I am a sensitive person.

_____18. I have flashbacks connected to those I help.

_____19. I have good peer support when I need to work through a highly stressful experience.

_____20. I have had first-hand experience with traumatic events in my adult life.

_____21. I have had first-hand experience with traumatic events in my childhood.

_____22. I think that I need to "work through" a traumatic experience in my life.

_____23. I think that I need more close friends.

_____24. I think that there is no one to talk with about highly stressful experiences.

_____25. I have concluded that I work too hard for my own good.

_____26. Working with those I help brings me a great deal of satisfaction.

_____27. I feel invigorated after working with those I help.

_____28. I am frightened of things a person I helped has said or done to me.

_____29. I experience troubling dreams similar to those I help.

_____30. I have happy thoughts about those I help and how I could help them.

_____31. I have experienced intrusive thoughts of times with especially difficult people I helped.

_____32. I have suddenly and involuntarily recalled a frightening experience while working with a person I helped.

_____33. I am pre-occupied with more than one person I help.

_____34. I am losing sleep over a person I help's traumatic experiences.

_____35. I have joyful feelings about how I can help the victims I work with.

_____36. I think that I might have been "infected" by the traumatic stress of those I help.

_____37. I think that I might be positively "inoculated" by the traumatic stress of those I help.

_____38. I remind myself to be less concerned about the well being of those I help.

_____39. I have felt trapped by my work as a helper.

_____40. I have a sense of hopelessness associated with working with those I help.

_____41. I have felt "on edge" about various things and I attribute this to working with certain people I help.

_____42. I wish that I could avoid working with some people I help.

_____43. Some people I help are particularly enjoyable to work with.

_____44. I have been in danger working with people I help.

_____45. I feel that some people I help dislike me personally.

Items about Being a Helper and Your Helping Environment

_____46. I like my work as a helper.

_____47. I feel like I have the tools and resources that I need to do my work as a helper.

_____48. I have felt weak, tired, run down as a result of my work as helper.

_____49. I have felt depressed as a result of my work as a helper.

_____50. I have thoughts that I am a "success" as a helper.

_____51. I am unsuccessful at separating helping from personal life.

_____52. I enjoy my co-workers.

_____53. I depend on my co-workers to help me when I need it.

_____54. My co-workers can depend on me for help when they need it.

_____55. I trust my co-workers.

_____56. I feel little compassion toward most of my co-workers.

_____57. I am pleased with how I am able to keep up with helping technology.

_____58. I feel I am working more for the money/prestige than for personal fulfillment.

_____59. Although I have to do paperwork that I don't like, I still have time to work with those I help.

_____60. I find it difficult separating my personal life from my helper life.

_____61. I am pleased with how I am able to keep up with helping techniques and protocols.

_____62. I have a sense of worthlessness/disillusionment/resentment associated with my role as a helper.

_____63. I have thoughts that I am a "failure" as a helper.

_____64. I have thoughts that I am not succeeding at achieving my life goals.

_____65. I have to deal with bureaucratic, unimportant tasks in my work as a helper.

_____66. I plan to be a helper for a long time.

Last updated 3/12/2002 11:21 P.M.

Suggested Reference: Stamm, B. H. & Figley, C. R. (1996). *Compassion Satisfaction and Fatigue Test. Available on the the World Wide Web:* http://www.isu.edu/~bhstamm/tests.htm.

Scoring Instructions

Please note that research is ongoing on this scale and the following scores should be used as a guide, not confirmatory information.
- Be certain you respond to all items.
- Mark the items for scoring:
  - Put an x by the following 26 items: 1–3, 5, 9–11, 14, 19, 26–27, 30, 35, 37, 43, 46–47, 50, 52–55, 57, 59, 61, 66.
  - Put a check by the following 16 items: 17, 23–25, 41, 42, 45, 48, 49, 51, 56, 58, 60, 62–65.
  - Circle the following 23 items: 4, 6–8, 12, 13, 15, 16, 18, 20–22, 28, 29, 31–34, 36, 38–40, 44.
- Add the numbers you wrote next to the items for each set of items and note:
  - Your potential for Compassion Satisfaction (x): 118 and above=extremely high potential; 100–117=high potential; 82–99=good potential; 64–81=modest potential; below 63=low potential.
- Your risk for Burnout (check): 36 or less=extremely low risk; 37–50=moderate risk; 51–75=high risk; 76–85=extremely high risk.
- Your risk for Compassion Fatigue (circle): 26 or less=extremely low risk, 27–30=low risk; 31–35=moderate risk; 36–40=high risk; 41 or more=extremely high risk.

Professional Resource Information

NOTE: URLs are given beside references rather than linked to the document name so that they can be read from print copy. While online, if you would like to link to a particular resource, click on the URL.

The Compassion Fatigue Scale has been established, presented, and published in several articles/chapters including, among others, the following:

Clemens, Lisa Ace. 1999. Secondary traumatic stress in rape crisis counselors: a descriptive study [thesis]. California State University, Fresno, M.S. thesis; Masters Abstracts 37/06: 1965.

Figley, C.R. 1998. Burnout as systemic traumatic stress: A model for helping traumatized family members. In *Burnout in families: The systemic costs of caring*, ed. C.R. Figley, 15–28. Boca Raton, Fla.: CRC Press.

Figley, C.R. 1995. *Compassion fatigue: Coping with secondary traumatic stress disorder in those who treat the traumatized.* New York: Brunner Mazel. *http://www.opengroup.com/open/dfbooks/087/0876307594.shtml.*

———. 1999. Compassion fatigue. In *Secondary traumatic stress: Self-care issues for clinicians, researchers and educators,* 2d ed., ed. B.H. Stamm. Lutherville, Md.: Sidran Press. *http://www.sidran.org/digicart/products/stss.html.*

Garrett, Carol. 1999. Stress, coping, empathy, secondary traumatic stress, and burnout in healthcare providers working with HIV-infected individuals. Doctoral diss. New York University. Dissertation Abstracts International 60/04-A: 1329.

Good, D.A. 1996. Secondary traumatic stress in art therapists and related mental health professionals. Doctoral diss. University of New Mexico. Dissertation Abstracts International 57/06-A: 2370.

Landry, L.P. 1999. Secondary traumatic stress disorder in the therapists from the Oklahoma City bombing. Diss. University of North Texas.

Ortlepp, K., and M. Friedman. 2001. The relationship between sense of coherence and indicators of secondary traumatic stress in non-professional trauma counsellors. *South African Journal of Psychology* (31) 2: 38–45.

Rudolph, J.M, B.H. Stamm,and H.E. Stamm. 1997. Compassion fatigue: A concern for mental health policy, providers and administration. Poster presented at the 13th Annual Conference of the International Society for Traumatic Stress Studies, Montreal, ON, CA. *http://www.isu.edu/~bhstamm/ISTSS97cf.PDF.* November.

Salston, M.G. 2000. Secondary traumatic stress: A study exploring empathy and the exposure to the traumatic material of survivors of community violence. Diss. The Florida State University.

Stamm, B.H. In press. Measuring compassion satisfaction as well as fatigue: Developmental history of the compassion fatigue and satisfaction test. In *Treating compassion fatigue,* ed. C.R. Figley. Philadelphia: Brunner/Mazel.

Stamm, B.H. 1997. Mental health research in telehealth. Invited address at From Research to Practice: A Conference on Rural Mental Health Research, National Institute of Mental Health. Oxford, Miss. April.

White, Geoffry D. 1998. Trauma treatment training for Bosnian and Croatian mental health workers. *American Journal of Orthopsychiatry* 68 (1): 58–62.

There is a psychometric review in:

Figley, C.R., and B.H. Stamm. 1996. Psychometric review of compassion fatigue self test. *http://www.isu.edu/~bhstamm/pdf/figleystamm.pdf.* In *Measurement of stress, trauma and adaptation,* ed. B.H. Stamm. Lutherville, Md.: Sidran Press *http://www.sidran.org/dicart/products/stss/html.*

For general information on Secondary Traumatic Stress/Vicarious Traumatization/Compassion Fatigue:

Pearlman, L., et al. 2000. Traumatic Stress Institute and Center for Adult and Adolescent Psychotherapy, LLC. *http://www.tsicaap.com.*

Pearlman, L., et al. 1999. *Risking connections.* Sidran Press. *http://www.riskingconnection.com/.*

Pearlman, L. , and K. Saakvitne. 1995. *Trauma and the therapist: Counter-transference and vicarious traumatization in psychotherapy with incest survivors.* New York: W.W. Norton. *http://web.wwnorton.com/catnos/ tl070183.htm.*

Figley, C.R. 1998. Traumatology E-Journal web site. *http://psy.uq.edu.au/ PTSD/trauma/j1.html.*

Stamm, B.H. 1999. *Secondary traumatic stress: Self-care issues for clinicians, researchers and educators,* 2d ed. Lutherville, Md.: Sidran Press. *http://www.sidran.org/digicart/products/ stss.html.*

Stamm, B.H. 1999. Creating virtual community: Telehealth and self-care updated. In *Secondary traumatic stress: Self-care issues for clinicians, researchers and educators,* 2d ed., ed. B.H. Stamm. Lutherville, Md.: Sidran Press. *http://www.isu.edu/ ~bhstamm/vircom.htm.*

Stamm, B.H. 1997. Work-related secondary traumatic stress. *PTSD Research Quarterly* (8)2, Spring. *http://www.isu.edu/dms/ptsd/RQ_ Spring_1997.html.*

———. 1997. Work-related secondary traumatic stress (reprint). Anxiety Disorders Association of America Reporter. Summer/Fall.

———. 1998. Rural-care: Crossroads of Health Care, Culture, Traumatic Stress and Technology. *http://www.isu.edu/~bhstamm/ index.htm.*

———. 1998. Traumatic stress secondary traumatic stress. *http://www.isu.edu/~bhstamm/ts.*

The psychometric information reported here is based on a pooled sample of 370 people. Multivariate analysis of variance did not provide evidence of differences based on country of origin, type of work, or sex when age was used as a control variable.

Age	Sex	Type of Work	Country of Origin
Mean 35.4	Males n=121 (33%)	Trauma Professional n=58 (16%)	USA Rural-Urban mix n=160 (43%)
Median 36	Females n=207 (56%)	Business volunteer n=130 (35%)	Canada-Urban n=30 (8%)
SD 12.16	Unknown n=42 (11%)	Red Cross n=30 (8%)	South Africa-Urban n=130 (35%)
		Caregivers in training n=102 (27%)	Internet (unknown origin) n=50 (13%)

Scale	Alpha	Mean	Standard Deviation	Interpretation
Compassion Satisfaction	.87	92.10	16.04	Higher is better satisfaction with ability to caregiver (e.g., pleasure to help, like colleagues, feel good about ability to help, make contribution, etc.)
Burnout	.90	24.18	10.78	Higher is higher risk for burnout (feel hopeless and unwilling to deal with work, onset gradual as a result of feeling one's efforts make no difference or very high workload)
Compassion Fatigue	.87	28.78	13.15	Higher is higher risk for Compassion Fatigue (symptoms of work-related PTSD, onset rapid as a result of exposure to highly stressful caregiving)

Additional Information: Lay Mental Health Caregivers in Rural Africa (n=16) (note, compassion satisfaction subscale was not given).
First assessment   (min 3 months work) CF Mean 45 (SD 14.4)   BO Mean 32   (SD 11.3)
Second assessment (3 months later)   CF Mean 44 (SD 13.6) BO Mean 28.86 (SD 9.6)

Here is the SPSS Scoring Code

```
COMPUTE Comsat=SUM( 1, 2, 3, 5, 9, 10, 11, 14, 19, 26, 27, 30, 35,
37, 43, 46, 47, 50, 52, 53, 54, 55, 57, 59, 61, 66)
COMPUTE Brnout=SUM(17, 23,24, 25, 41, 42, 45, 48, 49, 51, 56, 58,
60, 62, 63, 64, 65)
COMPUTE ComFat=SUM( 4, 6, 7, 8, 12, 13, 15, 16, 18, 20, 21, 22, 28,
29, 31, 32, 33, 34, 36, 38, 39, 40, 44)
```

Literature Cited

Aguilera, D.C. 1995. *Crisis intervention: Theory and methodology.* St. Louis, Mo.: Mosby.

Antony, J.S. 1998. Personality-career fit and freshman medical career aspirations. *Research in High Education* 39(6): 679–698.

American Veterinary Medical Association. 1998. Definition of the human-animal bond. *Journal of the American Veterinary Medical Association.* June 1. Found at Argus Institute for Families and Veterinary Medicine. Colorado State University. *www.argusinstitute.colostate.edu/define/htm.*

Barker, S. 1999. Therapeutic aspects of the human-companion animal interaction. *Psychiatric Times* 16(2). *www.psychiatrictimes.com.*

Barnes, M.F. 2004. When a child is traumatized or physically injured: The secondary trauma of parents. In *Specific stressors: Interventions with couples and families,* ed. D.R. Catherall. New York: Brunner-Routledge.

Beaver, B. 2003. A global survey of the human-animal bond. *JAVMA News,* September 15, 1. *www.avma.org/onlnews/javma/sept03.*

Boscarino, J.A. 2004. Association between PTSD and physical illness: Results and implications from clinical epidemiological studies. *Annals of the New York Academy of Sciences* 1032: 141–153.

Boscarino, J.A., C.R. Figley, and R.E. Adams. 2004. Evidence of compassion fatigue following the September 11 terrorist attacks: A study of secondary trauma among social workers in New York. *International Journal of Emergency Mental Health* 6(2): 98–108.

Braun, G.L. 1996. The impact of a stress reduction program on psychological distress and occupational self-esteem for animal care workers. PhD diss., University of Cincinnati.

Cerney, M.S. 1995. Treating the "heroic treaters." In *Compassion fatigue,* ed. C.R. Figley, 131–148. New York: Brunner/Mazel.

Collord, R. 1988. Euthanasia workshops: Dealing with employee relationships, too. *Shelter Sense,* April, 11.

Crimi, M. 1998. Foreword. In *Connecting with clients: Practical communication techniques for 15 common situations*, ed. L. Lagoni, D. Durrance, 9. Lakewood, Colo.: AAHA Press.

Danieli, Y. 1996. Who takes care of the caregiver? In *Minefields in their hearts*, ed. R.J. Apfel and B. Simon, 189–205. New Haven, Conn.: Yale University Press.

Dollard, M.F., T. Winefield, and H.R. Winefield, eds. 2003. *Occupational stress in the service professions*. London: CRC Press.

Dutton, M.A., and F.L. Rubinstein. 1995. Working with people with PTSD: Research implications. In *Compassion fatigue*, ed. C.R. Figley, 82–100. New York: Brunner/Mazel.

Etzion, D. 1984. Moderating effect of social support on the stress-burnout relationships. *Journal of Applied Psychology* 69(4): 615–622.

Fakkema. D. 1991. The four phases. *Animal Sheltering*, Mar-April. www.animalsheltering.org/resource_library/magazine_articles/mar_apr_2001/four_phases.html.

Farber, B.A. 1983a. Dysfunctional aspects of the psychotherapeutic role. In *Stress and burnout in the human service professions*, ed. B.A. Farber, 97–118. New York: Pergamon Press.

———. 1983b. Introduction: A critical perspective on burnout. In *Stress and burnout in the human service professions*, ed. B.A. Farber, 1–20. New York: Pergamon Press.

Figley, C.R. 1982. Traumatization and comfort: Close relationships may be hazardous to your health. Keynote presentation at "Families and Close Relationships: Individuals in Social Interaction," conference. Texas Tech University, Lubbock, Tex., February.

———. 1993. Coping with stressors on the home front. *Journal of Social Issues* 49(4): 51–71.

———. 1995. Compassion fatigue as secondary traumatic stress disorder: An overview. In *Compassion fatigue: Coping with secondary traumatic stress disorder*, ed. C.R. Figley, 1–20. New York: Brunner/Mazel.

———, ed. 1999. *Traumatology of grieving: Conceptual, theoretical, and treatment foundations*. Philadelphia: Taylor and Francis.

———. 2001. Compassionate heart and compassion fatigue. Workshop, Phoebe Putney Memorial Hospital Behavioral Health Center, Albany, Ga., July 20.

———, ed. 2002. *Treating compassion fatigue*. New York: Brunner-Routledge.

Fucco, L.W. 2002. Pet tails. *Post-Gazette.com/pets*, Dec. 31, 1.

Furstenberg, A. 1978. *Burnout.* New York: Academic Press.

Gentry, J.E., and T. Zaparaneck. 2003. Compassion fatigue in animal-related fields: Peer-to-peer accelerated recover techniques. Workshop script and handout. Sponsored by the Kenneth A. Scott Charitable Trust and The HSUS.

Gentry, J.E., A. Baranowsky, and K. Dunning. 2002. Accelerated recovery program for compassion fatigue. Paper presented at the meeting of the International Society for Traumatic Stress Studies, Montreal, Quebec, Canada. November.

Gilerton, M.W., M.E. Shenton, A. Ciszewski, K. Kasi, N.B. Lasko, S.P. Orr, and R.K. Pitman. 2002. Smaller hippocampal volume predicts pathologic vulnerability to psychological trauma. *Nature Neuroscience* 5: 1242–1247.

Gilman, N., and J. Shepherd. 1992. Misanthropy and anthropomorphism: Two ten dollar words and how to manage them. *Shelter Sense,* August, 8.

Hayes, J.A., C.J. Gelso, S.L. Van Wagoner, and R.A. Diemer. 1991. Managing countertransference: What the experts think. *Psychological Reports* 69: 139–148.

Henderson, C.E. 2003. *Self hypnosis: For the life you want.* New York: Biocentrix Publishing.

Hilfiker, D. 1985. *Healing the wounds: A physician looks at his work.* New York: Pantheon.

Hollingsworth, M.A. 1993. Responses of female therapists to treating adult female survivors of incest. Doctoral diss., Western Michigan University. *Dissertation Abstracts International.*

The Humane Society of the United States (HSUS). 2003–2004. Compassion satisfaction/Fatigue self-test: Animal care. Adapted with permission from C.R. Figley. 1995. *Compassion fatigue: Coping with secondary traumatic stress disorder.* Washington, D.C.: HSUS.

Humane Society University. 2001. Leadership development for animal care and control professionals. Workshop and handout. Morristown, N.J. May. Chapter 5: 5.

Jacobs, M. 1991. The therapist's revenge. The law of Talion as a motive for caring. *Interdisciplinary Journal of Pastoral Studies* 105: 2–11.

Janoff-Bulman, R. 1989. Assumptive worlds and the stress of traumatic events: Applications of the schema construct. *Social Cognition* 7(2): 113–136.

Jenkins, S.R., and S. Baird. 2002. Secondary traumatic stress and vicarious trauma: A validational study.

Journal of Trauma Stress 15(5): 423–432.

Joinson, C. 1992. Coping with compassion fatigue. *Nursing* 22(4): 116–122.

Kassam-Adams, N. 1999. The risks of treating sexual trauma: Stress and secondary trauma in psychotherapists. In *Secondary traumatic stress: Self-care issues for clinicians, researchers, and educators,* ed. B.H. Stamm, 37–48. Towson, Md.: Sidran Institute.

Koerner, J. 1995. The essence of nursing–Creative compassion. *Journal of Professional Nursing* 11(6): 317, 366.

Lee, C.S. 1995. Secondary traumatic stress in therapists who are exposed to client traumatic material. Doctoral diss., Florida State University. *Dissertation Abstracts International.*

Luechefeld, L. 2005. The balancing act: A new life skill. *Veterinary Practice News* 17(2): 10–11.

Manette, C. 2004. A reflection on the ways veterinarians cope with death, euthanasia, and slaughter of animals. *Journal of American Veterinary Medicine* 225(1): 34–38.

Maslach, C. 1982. Understanding burnout: Definitional issues in analyzing a complex phenomenon. In *Job stress and burnout: Research, theory and intervention perspectives,* ed. W.S. Paine, 29–40. Beverly Hills, Calif.: Sage Publications.

Maslach, C., and M.P. Leiter. 1997. *The truth about burnout.* San Francisco: Jossey Bass Publishers.

McCann, I.L., and L.A. Pearlman. 1990. Vicarious traumatization: A framework for understanding the psychological effects of working with victims. *Journal of Traumatic Stress* 3(1): 131–149.

Merriam-Webster. 2002. *Medical desk dictionary*, rev. ed. New York: Merriam Publishers.

Mitchener, K.L., and G.K. Ogilvie. 2002. Understanding CF: Keys for the caring veterinary healthcare team. *Journal of the American Animal Hospital Association* 38(4): 307–310.

Muss, D.C. 2002. The rewind technique in the treatment of PTSD: Methods and applications. In *Brief treatments for the traumatized: A project of the Green Cross Foundation,* ed. C.R. Figley, 306–314. Westport, Conn.: Greenwood Press.

Neumann, D.A., and S.J. Gamble. 1995. Issues in the professional development of psychotherapists: Countertransference and vicarious traumatization in the new trauma therapist. *Psychotherapy* 32(2): 341–347.

NiCarthy, G., K. Merriam, and S. Coffman. 1984. *Talking it out: A guide to groups for abused women.* Seattle: Seal Press.

PAWSitive Inter Action. 2002. A scientific look at the human-animal bond. Atlanta, Ga.: PAWSitive Inter Action. *www.pawsitiveinteraction.org.*

———. 2003. Pets and the aging: Science supports the human-animal bond. Atlanta, Ga.: PAWSitive Inter Action. *www.pawsitiveinteraction.org.*

Pearlman, L.A., and P.S. MacIan. 1995. Vicarious traumatization: An empirical study of the effects of trauma work on trauma therapists. *Professional Psychology: Research and Practice* 26(6): 558–563.

Pearlman, L.A., and K.W. Saakvitne. 1995. Treating therapists with vicarious traumatization and secondary traumatic stress disorders. In *Compassion fatigue,* ed. C.R. Figley,

150–177. New York: Brunner/Mazel.

Pines, A., and E. Aronson. 1988. *Career burnout: Causes and cures.* New York: The Free Press.

Prosser, D., S. Johnson, E. Kupers, G. Szmukler, P. Bebbington, and G. Thorncroft. 1996. Mental health, "burnout," and job satisfaction among hospital and community-based mental health staff. *British Journal of Psychiatry* 169: 334–337.

Regehr, C., and J.A. Hill. 2002. Crisis debriefings for emergency service workers. In *Brief treatments for the traumatized: A project of the Green Cross Foundation,* ed. C.R. Figley, 292–306. London: Greenwood Press.

Robbins, S., ed. 2005. *Organization behavior,* 11h ed., Upper Saddle River, N.J: Pearson/Prentice Hall.

Roop, R., and D.M. Vitelli. 2003. Compassion fatigue in the animal care field. Selected papers from the 21st NWRA symposium, ed. B. Orendorff. *Wildlife Rehabilitation* 21: 146–147.

Ross, M. 1988. *The wellness workbook.* Travis, Md.: Ten Speed Press.

Sabin-Farrel, R., and G. Turpin. 2003. Vicarious traumatization: Implications for the mental health of health workers? *Clinical Psychology Review* May 23(3): 449–480.

Salston, M.D., and C.R. Figley. 2003. Secondary traumatic stress effects of working with survivors of criminal victimization. *Journal of Traumatic Stress* 16(1): 167–174.

Samantrai, K. 1992. Factors in the decision to leave: Retaining social workers with MSWs in public child welfare. *Social Work* 37: 454–458.

Schauben, L.J., and P.A. Frazier. 1995. Vicarious trauma: The effects on female counselors of working with sexual violence survivors. *Psychology of Women Quarterly* 19: 49–64.

Smith, W.H. 1990. Euthanasia: The human factor. HSUS training program. Unpublished manuscript. Washington, D.C.: The Humane Society of the United States.

Soares, C. 2005. The balancing act: A new life skill. *Veterinary Practice News* 17(2): 11.

Stamm, B.H. 2002. Compassion fatigue/Compassion satisfaction scale. Traumatic Stress Research Group. *http://www.dartmouth.edu/~bhstamm/pd f/satfa.pdf.*

Stav, A., V. Florian, and E.Z. Shurka. 1987. Burnout among social workers working with physically disabled persons and bereaved families. *Journal of Social Service Research* 10: 81–93.

Sze, W.C., and B. Ivker. 1986. Stress in social workers: The impact of setting and role. *Social Casework* 67: 141–148.

Tai, T.W.C., S.I. Bame, and C.D. Robinson. 1998. Review of nursing turnover research, 1977–1996. *Social Science and Medicine* 47(12): 1905–1924.

Tillett, R. 2003. The patient within: Psychopathology professions. *Psychiatric Treatment* 9: 272–279.

Todd, C.M., and D.M. Deery-Schmitt. 1996. Factors affecting turnover among family child care providers: A longitudinal study. *Early Childhood Research Quarterly* 11(3): 351–376.

Tracy, E.M., N. Beam, S. Gwatkin, and B. Hill. 1992. Family preservation workers: Sources of job satisfaction and job stress. *Research on Social Work Practice* 2(4): 465–478.

Valent, P. 2002. Diagnosis and treatment of helper stresses, traumas, and illness. In *Treating compassion fatigue,* ed. C.R. Figley, 17–38. New York: Brunner-Routledge.

Vermont Veterinary Medical Association. n.d. Animal health care questions and answers. *www.vtvets. org/htm/faz/friendship.htm.*

Vogel, T. 2004. The weight of compassion. *www.vetcentric.com.*

Wagner, T. 2000. Animals in our hearts: Balancing service and self care. *www.animalsinourhearts.com.*

White, D. 1998. It's a dog's life–Animal shelter workers share the psychological impact of having to euthanize animals as part of their daily routine. *Psychology Today,* November–December.

Wikipedia. n.d. *http://en.wikipedia.org/wiki/.*

Winiarskyj, L. 2001. Kindness to people and animals: Are they connected? *Kind Teacher.* E. Haddam, Conn.: The National Association for Humane and Environmental Education.

Bibliography

Acker, G.M. 1999. The impact of clients' mental illness on social workers' job satisfaction and burnout. *Health and Social Work* 24(2): 112–119.

Aiken M., and J. Hage. 1968. Organizational interdependence and intraorganizational structure. *American Sociological Review* 33: 912–930.

Allen, N.J., and J.P. Meyer. 1990. The measurements and antecedents of affective, continuance, and normative commitment to the organization. *Journal of Occupational and Organizational Psychology* 63(1): 1–19.

American Humane Association (AHA). 2000. SB2030 child welfare services workload study. Final report. Englewood, Colo.: AHA. April.

American Public Human Services Association (APHSA). 2001. Report from the child welfare workforce survey: State and county data and findings. Washington, D.C.: APHSA.

Arches, J. 1991. Social structure, burnout, and job satisfaction. *Social Work* 36(3): 202–206.

Balfour, D.L., and D.M. Neff. 1993. Predicting and managing turnover in human services agencies: A case study of an organization in crisis. *Public Personnel Management* 22(3): 473–86.

Bandura, A. 1977. Self-efficacy: Toward a unifying theory of behavioral change. *Psychological Review* 84(2): 191–215.

———. 1989. Human agency in social cognitive theory. *American Psychologist* 44(9): 1175–1184.

Bandura, A., and R. Wood. 1989. Effect of perceived controllability and performance standards on self-regulation of complex decision making. *Journal of Personality and Social Psychology* 56(5): 805–814.

Barrett, M.C., and J. McKelvey. 1980. Stresses and strains on the child care worker: Typologies for assessment. *Child Welfare* 59(5): 277–285.

Barth, M.C. 2003. Social work labor market: A first look. *Social Work* 48(1): 9–19.

Ben-Dror, R. 1994. Employee turnover in community mental health organization: A developmental stages study.

Community Mental Health Journal 30(3): 243–257.

Best Places. 2001. *http://www.bestplaces.net.*

Biggerstaff, M.A., and M.S. Kolevzon. 1980. Differential use of social work knowledge, skills, and techniques by MSW, BSW, and BA level practitioners. *Journal of Education for Social Work* 16(3): 67–74.

Blankertz, L., and S. Robinson. 1996. Turnover intentions of community mental health workers in psychosocial rehabilitation services. *Community Mental Health Journal* 33(6): 517–529.

Burton, L., and D. Goldsmith. 2002. The medium is the message: Using online focus groups to study online learning. Hartford, Conn.: Association for Intuitional Research, Connecticut Distance Learning Consortium. June.

Butler, B.B. 1990. Job satisfaction: Management's continuing challenge. *Social Work* 35(2): 112–117.

California Employment Development Department. 2001. *http://www.calmis.cahwnet.gov.*

California Social Work Education Center. 1996. The retention study questionnaire: Factors influencing the retention of public child welfare workers. Berkeley, Calif.: California Social Work Education Center.

————. 1999. 1999 annual report: Focusing on public social services. Berkeley, Calif.: California Social Work Education Center.

Cammann, C., M. Fichman, D. Jenkins, and J. Klesh. 1979. The Michigan organizational assessment question- naire. Unpublished manuscript, University of Michigan, Ann Arbor.

Cauble, A.E., and L.P. Thurston. 2000. Effects of interactive multimedia training on knowledge, attitudes, and self-efficacy of social work students. *Research on Social Work Practice* 10(4): 48–57.

Children Now. 2001. California county data book. *http://www.childrennow.org.*

Clark, S. 2002. *Literature review for retention.* For the California Department of Social Services Human Resources Subcommittee. Berkeley, Calif.: California Social Work Education Center. February.

Council of Family and Child Caring Agencies. 1989. *Who will care for the children? A report on the work force crisis in child welfare.* New York: Council of Family and Child Caring Agencies.

Daly, D., D. Dudley, D. Finnegan, L. Jones, and L. Christiansen. 2000. Staffing child welfare services in the new millennium. San Diego, Calif.: Network for Excellence in Human Services. June.

Deci, E.L. 1995. *Why we do what we do: The dynamics of personal autonomy.* New York: Putnam's Sons.

Dhooper, S.S., D.D. Royse, and L.C. Wolfe. 1990. Does social work education make a difference? *Social Work* 35(1): 57–61.

Dickinson, N.S., and R. Perry. 2002. Do MSW graduates stay in public child welfare? Factors influencing the burnout and retention rates of specially educated child welfare workers. *Journal of Health and Social Policy* 15(1/2).

Dillman, D.D. 2000. *Mail and Internet surveys: The tailored design method,* 2d ed. New York: Wiley.

Drake, B., and G.N. Yadama. 1996. A structural equation model of burnout and job exit among child protective service workers. *Social Work Research* 20(3): 179–187.

Dressel, P.L. 1982. Policy sources of worker dissatisfactions: The case of human services in aging. *Social Service Review* 56(3): 406–423.

Dubey, S.N., and Y. Meller. 1988. Relationships among task complexity, structure, job performance and satisfaction in social service organizations. *The Indian Journal of Social Work* 49(4): 321–336.

DuBrin, A.J. 2001. Career-related correlates of self-discipline. *Psychological Reports* 89(1): 107–110.

Ellett, A.J. 2000. Human caring, self-efficacy beliefs, and professional organizational culture correlates of employee retention in child welfare. Unpublished doctoral diss., Louisiana State University, Baton Rouge.

—————. 2001. Organizational culture and intent to remain employed in child welfare: A two-state study. Dallas, Tex.: Council on Social Work Education Annual Program Meeting.

—————. 2001. Self-efficacy beliefs and employee retention in child welfare: A multi-state study. Dallas, Tex.: Council on Social Work Education Annual Program Meeting.

Ellett, A.J., C.D. Ellett, and J.K. Rugutt. 2003. A study of personal and organizational factors contributing to employee retention and turnover in child welfare in Georgia: Final project report. School of Social Work, University of Georgia. June.

Ewalt, P.L. 1991. Trends affecting recruitment and retention of social work staff in human service agencies. *Social Work* 36(3): 214–217.

Furman, W. 1998. Retention of stipended IUC MSW students in the Los Angeles County Department of Children and Family Services. Los Angeles: Inter-University Consortium, Department of Social Welfare, UCLA. June.

Gaiser, T.J. 1997. Conducting online focus groups: A methodological discussion. *Social Science Computer Review* 15(2): 135–144.

Gibelman, M. 1998. Women's perceptions of the glass ceiling in human service organizations and what to do about it. *Affilia: Journal of Women and Social Work* 13(2): 147–165.

Gibelman, M., and P.H. Schervish. 1995. Pay equity in social work: Not! *Social Work* 40(5): 622–630.

Giles, M., and A. Rea. 1999. Career self-efficacy: An application of the theory of planned behaviour. *Journal of Occupational and Organizational Psychology* 72(3): 393–398.

Gist, M.E. 1989. The influence of training method on self-efficacy and idea generation among managers. *Personnel Psychology* 42(1): 787–805.

Gleason-Wynn, P. 1995. Improving job satisfaction, retention among nursing home social workers. *Brown University Long-Term Care Letter* 7(3): 1–3.

Gleeson, J.P., J.H. Smith, and A.C. Dubois. 1993. Developing child welfare practitioners: Avoiding the single-solution seduction. *Administration in Social Work* 17(3): 21–37.

Glisson, C., and M. Durick. 1988. Predictors of job satisfaction and organizational commitment in human service organizations. *Administrative Science Quarterly* 33: 61–81.

Glisson, C., and A. Hemmelgarn. 1998. The effects of organizational climate and interorganizational coordination on the quality and outcomes of children's service systems. *Child Abuse and Neglect* 22(5): 401–421.

Graef, M.I., and E.L. Hill. 2000. Costing child protective services staff turnover. *Child Welfare* 79(5): 517–533.

Guterman, N.B., and D. Bargal. 1996. Social workers' perceptions of their power and service outcomes. *Administration in Social Work* 20(3): 1–20.

Gutierrez, L., and L. GlenMaye. 1995. The organizational context of empowerment practice: Implications for social work administrators. *Social Work* 40(2): 249–258.

Hage, J., and M. Aiken. 1969. Routine technology, social structure and organizational goals. *Administrative Science Quarterly* 14: 366–376.

Halaby, C.N. 1986. Worker attachment and workplace authority. *American Sociological Review* 51: 634–649.

Harrington, D., N. Bean, D. Pintello, and D. Mathews. 2001. Job satisfaction and burnout: Predictors of intentions to leave a job in a military setting. *Administration in Social Work* 25(3): 1–16.

Hegar, R.L., and J.M. Hunzeker. 1988. Moving toward empowerment-based practice in public child welfare. *Social Work* 33(6): 499–502.

Helfgott, K.P. 1991. *Staffing the child welfare agency: Recruitment and retention.* Washington, D.C.: Child Welfare League of America.

Henry, S. 1990. Non-salary retention incentives for social workers in public mental health. *Administration in Social Work* 14(3): 1–15.

Hopkins, K.M., and N.R. Mudrick. 1999. Impact of university/agency partnerships in child welfare on organizations, workers, and work activities. *Child Welfare* 78(6): 749–774.

Horejsi, C., and C. Garthwait. 1994. A survey of threats and violence directed against child protection workers in a rural state. *Child Welfare* 73(2): 173–179.

Huber, R., and B.P. Orlando. 1995. Persisting gender differences in social workers' incomes: Does the profession really care? *Social Work* 40(5): 585–592.

Hui, C.H. 1988. Impacts of objective and subjective labour market conditions on employee turnover. *Journal of Occupational Psychology* 61(3): 211–219.

Hulin, C.L., M. Roznowski, and D. Hachiya. 1985. Alternative opportunities and withdrawal decisions: Empirical and theoretical discrepancies and integration. *Psychological Bulletin* 97(2): 233–250.

Iverson, R.D., and D.B. Currivan. 2003. Union participation, job satisfaction, and employee turnover: An event-history analysis of the exit-voice hypothesis. *Industrial Relations* 42(1): 101–105.

Jayaratne, S., and W.A. Chess. 1984. Job satisfaction, burnout, and turnover: A national study. *Social Work* 29(5): 448–453.

———. 1986. Job satisfaction: A comparison of caseworkers and administrators. *Social Work* 31(2): 144–146.

———. 1991. Job satisfaction and burnout: Is there a difference? *Journal of Applied Social Sciences* 15: 245–262.

Jayaratne, S., W.A. Chess, and D.A Kunkel. 1986. Burnout: Its impact on child welfare workers and their spouses. *Social Work* 31(1): 53–59.

Jex, S.M. 1998. *Stress and job performance: Theory, research, and implications for managerial practice.* Thousand Oaks, Calif.: Sage Publications, Inc.

Jinnett, K., and J.A. Alexander. 1999. The influence of organizational context on quitting intention: An examination of treatment staff in long-term mental health care settings. *Research on Aging* 21(2): 176–204.

Jones, L., and A. Okamura. 2000. Reprofessionalizing child welfare services: An evaluation of a Title IV-E training program. *Research on Social Work Practice* 10(5): 607–621.

Joseph, M.V., and A.P. Conrad. 1989. Social work influence on interdisciplinary ethical decision making in health settings. *Health and Social Work* 14: 22–30.

Judge, T.A., and J.E. Bono. 2001. Relationship of core self-evaluation traits—self-esteem, generalized self-efficacy, locus of control, and emotional stability: A meta-analysis. *Journal of Applied Psychology* 86(1): 80–92.

Karger, H.J. 1989. The common and conflicting goals of labor and social work. *Administration in Social Work* 13(1): 1–17.

Kiesler, C.A. 1977. Sequential events in commitment. *Journal of Personality* 45(1): 65–78.

Kiyak, H.A., K.H. Namazi, and E.F. Kahana. 1997. Job commitment and turnover among women working in facilities serving older persons. *Research on Aging* 19(2): 223–246.

Koeske, G.F., and S.A. Kirk,. 1995. The effect of characteristics of human service workers on subsequent morale and turnover. *Administration in Social Work* 19(1): 15–31.

Krueger, M. 1996. *Job satisfaction for child and youth care workers,* 3d ed. Washington, D.C.: Child Welfare

League of America Press.

Lance, C.E. 1991. Evaluation of a structural model relating job satisfaction, organizational commitment, and precursors to voluntary turnover. *Multivariate Behavioral Research* 26(1): 137–162.

Landsman, M.J. 2001. Commitment in public child welfare. *Social Service Review* 75(3): 387–419.

Lawler, E.J. 2001. An affect theory of social exchange. *American Journal of Sociology* 107(2): 321–353.

Lee, R.T., and B.E. Ashforth. 1993. A longitudinal study of burnout among supervisors and managers: Comparisons between the Leiter and Maslach (1988) and Golembiewski et al. (1986) models. *Organizational Behavior and Human Decision Processes* 54: 369–398.

———. 1993. A further examination of managerial burnout: Toward an integrated model. *Journal of Organizational Behavior* 14: 3–20.

Lee, R., and E.R. Wilbur. 1985. Age, education, job tenure, salary, job characteristics, and job satisfaction: A multivariate analysis. *Human Relations* 38(8): 781–791.

Lee, T.W., T.R, Mitchell, B.C. Holtom, L.S. McDaniel, and J.W. Hill. 1999. The unfolding model of voluntary turnover: A replication and extension. *Academy of Management Journal* 42(4): 450–462.

Leiter, M. 1988. Burnout as a function of communication patterns. *Group and Organizational Studies* 13(1): 111–128.

Leslie, D.R., C.M. Holzhalb, and T.P. Holland. 1998. Measuring staff empowerment: Development of a worker empowerment scale. *Research on Social Work Practice* 8(2): 212–222.

Lieberman, A.A., H. Hornby, and M. Russell. 1988. Analyzing the educational backgrounds and work experiences of child welfare personnel: A national study. *Social Work* 3: 485–489.

Lincoln, J.R., and A.L. Kalleberg. 1990. *Culture, control, and commitment: A study of work organization and work attitudes in the United States and Japan.* Cambridge: Cambridge University Press.

March, J.G., and H.A. Simon. 1958. *Organizations.* New York: Wiley.

Maslach, C., and S.E. Jackson. 1984. Patterns of burnout among a national sample of public contact workers. *Journal of Health and Human Resources Administration* 7: 189–212.

Maslach, C., W.B. Schaufeli, and M.P. Leiter. 2001. Burnout. *Annual Review of Psychology* 52(1): 397–422.

McCloskey, J.C., and B.E. McCain. 1987. Satisfaction, commitment and professionalism of newly employed nurses. *Image: Journal of Nursing Scholarship* 19(1): 20–24.

McLean, J., and T. Andrew. 2000. Commitment, satisfaction, stress, and control among social service managers and social workers in the UK. *Administration in Social Work* 23(3/4): 93–117.

McNeely, R.L. 1984. Occupation, gender, and work satisfaction in a comprehensive human service department. *Administration in Social Work* 8(2): 35–47.

Michaels, C.E., and P.E. Spector. 1982. Causes of employee turnover: A test of the Mobley, Griffeth, Hand, and Meglino model. *Journal of Applied Psychology* 67(1): 53–59.

Miller, O. 1996. *Employee turnover in the public sector.* New York: Garland Publishing.

Mitchell, T.R., B.C. Holtom, T.W. Lee, C.J. Sablynski, and M. Erez. 2001.

Why people stay: Using job embeddedness to predict voluntary turnover. *Academy of Management Journal* 44(6): 1102–1121.

Mor Barak, M.E., J.A. Nissly, and A. Levin. 2001. Antecedents to retention and turnover among child welfare, social work, and other human service employees: What can we learn from past research? A review and meta-analysis. *Social Service Review* 75(3): 625–661.

Mueller, C.W., and E.M. Boyer. 1994. Employee attachment and non-coercive conditions of work: The case of dental hygienists. *Work and Occupations* 21(2): 179–212.

National Survey of Child and Adolescent Well-Being Research Group. 2001. National survey of child and adolescent well-being: Local child welfare agency survey. Washington, D.C.: Administration on Children, Youth, and Families.

Needell, B., D. Webster, A. Cuccaro-Alamin, M. Armijo, S. Lee, A. Brookhart, and B. Lery. 2001. Performance indicators for child welfare in California. *(http://cssr.berkeley.edu).*

Nesbary, D. 2000. *Survey research and the World Wide Web.* Boston: Allyn and Bacon.

Oldham, G.R., and J.R. Hackman. 1981. Relationships between organizational structure and employee reactions: Comparing alternative frameworks. *Administrative Science Quarterly* 26: 66–83.

Olsen, L., and W.M. Holmes. 1982. Educating child welfare workers: The effects of professional training on service delivery. *Journal of Education for Social Work* 18(1): 94–102.

O'Neill, J. 2000. Social work jobs

abound. *NASW News* 45(8).

Orthner, D.K., and J.F. Pittman. 1986. Family contributions to work commitment. *Journal of Marriage and the Family* 48(3): 573–581.

Pearlmutter, S. 1998. Self-efficacy and organizational change leadership. *Administration in Social Work* 22(3): 23–38.

Pecora, P.J., J.K. Whittaker, A.N. Maluccio, and R.P. Barth. 2000. *The child welfare challenge: Policy, practice, and research,* 2d ed. Hawthorne, N.Y.: Aldine de Gruyter.

Perry, R., G. Limb, and S. Clark. 1999. A report on the 1998 public child welfare workforce in California across training academy regions. Berkeley, Calif.: California Social Work Education Center.

Pines, A., and C. Maslach. 1978. Characteristics of staff burnout in mental health settings. *Hospital and Community Psychiatry* 29(4): 233–237.

Poulin, J.E. 1994. Job task and organizational predictors of social worker job satisfaction change: A panel study. *Administration in Social Work* 18(1): 21–38.

Poulin, J.E., and C. Walter. 1992. Retention plans and job satisfaction of gerontological social workers. *Journal of Gerontological Social Work* 19: 99–114.

Powell, M.J., and R.O. Yourk. 1992. Turnover in county public welfare agencies. *Journal of Applied Social Sciences* 16(2): 111–127.

Price, J.L. 1972. *Handbook of organizational measurement.* Lexington, Mass.: D.C. Heath and Company.

———. 1977. *The study of turnover.* Ames, Iowa: Iowa State University Press.

Ratliff, N. 1988. Stress and burnout in the helping professions. *Social Casework: The Journal of Contemporary Casework* 69(3): 14–154.

Reagh, R. 1994. Public child welfare professionals: Those who stay. *Journal of Sociology and Social Welfare* 32(3): 69–78.

Rittner, B., and J.S. Wodarski. 1999. Differential uses for BSW and MSW educated social workers in child welfare services. *Children and Youth Services Review* 21(3): 217–238.

Rizzo, J.R., R.J. House, and S.I. Lirtzman. 1970. Role conflict and ambiguity in complex organizations. *Administrative Science Quarterly* 15(2): 150–162.

Rycraft, J.R. 1994. The party isn't over: The agency role in the retention of public child welfare caseworkers. *Social Work* 39(1): 75–80.

Scalera, N.R. 1995. The critical need for specialized health and safety measures for child welfare workers. *Child Welfare* 74(2): 337–350.

Schneider, S.J., J. Kerwin, J. Frechtling, and B.A. Vivari. 2002. Characteristics of the discussion in online and face-to-face focus groups. *Social Science Computer Review* 20(1): 31–42.

Seaberg, J.R. 1982. Getting there from here: Revitalizing child welfare training. *Social Work* 27(5): 441–447.

Spector, P.E. 1997. *Job satisfaction: Application, assessment, causes, and consequences.* Newbury Park, Calif.: Sage Publications, Inc.

Staw, B.M., and J. Ross. 1985. Stability in the midst of change: A dispositional approach to job attitudes. *Journal of Applied Psychology* 70(3): 469–480.

U.S. General Accounting Office (GAO). 2003. HHS could plan a greater role in helping child welfare agencies recruit and retain staff. Washington, D.C.: GAO.

Vinokur-Kaplan, D. 1991. Job satisfaction among social workers in public and voluntary child welfare agencies. *Child Welfare* 70(1): 81–91.

Vinokur-Kaplan, D., S. Jayaratne, and W.A. Chess. 1994. Job satisfaction and retention of social workers in public agencies, non-profit agencies and private practice: The impact of workplace conditions and motivators. *Administration in Social Work* 18(3): 93–121.

Walston, J.T., and R.W. Lissitz. 2000. Computer-mediated focus groups. *Evaluation Review* 24(5): 457–483.

Weaver, D. 1999. The retention of stipended MSW graduates in a public child welfare agency. Los Angeles: USC School of Social Work, Center on Child Welfare. November.

Weiner, N. 1980. Determinants and behavioral consequences of pay satisfaction: A comparison of two models. *Personnel Psychology* 33(4): 741–757.

Williamson, D.A. 1996. *Job satisfaction in social services.* New York: Garland Publishing, Inc.

Zunz, S.J. 1998. Resiliency and burnout: Protective factors for human service managers. *Administration in Social Work* 22(3): 39–54.

Index

Page numbers in italics refer to tables or figures

B

C

T

V